FOLK HATS

Editor: Ann Budd
Technical Editor: Jean Lampe
Illustration: Vicki Square and Gayle Ford
Photography: Joe Coca
Photostyling: Ann Swanson
Cover and interior design: Susan Wasinger
Production: Pauline Brown
Proofreading and indexing: Nancy Arndt

Interweave Press LLC
201 East Fourth Street
Loveland, Colorado 80537-5655 USA
www.interweave.com

Printed in Singapore by Tien Wah Press (Pte) Limited

Library of Congress Cataloging-in-Publication Data

Square, Vicki, 1954–
  Folk hats : 32 knitting patterns and tales from around the world / Vicki Square.
    p. cm.
  Includes bibliographical references and index.
  ISBN 1-931499-63-2
  1. Knitting—Patterns. 2. Hats. I. Title.
  TT825.S7137 2005
  746.43'20432—dc22
                            2005003008

10 9 8 7 6 5 4 3 2 1

VICKI SQUARE

FOLK HATS

32 KNITTING PATTERNS & TALES FROM AROUND THE WORLD

INTERWEAVE PRESS
www.interweave.com

FOLK HATS

Contents

Introduction 6

Hat Basics 8

Hat Projects 12

North America
CANADA
   Deerstalker Hat 14
UNITED STATES
   Cowboy Hat 19
   Baseball Cap 22

South America
PERU
   Hut Hat 26
BOLIVIA
   Bolivian Derby 30
ECUADOR
   Panama Hat 33

Africa
CONGO
   Raffia Pillbox 36
NIGERIA
   Gourd Baby Bonnet . . . 40
   Yoruba Bird 43
CAMEROON
   Ruffled Dignity 47

Continental Europe
SPAIN
   Cordobes with Scarf . . . 51
ITALY
   Gondolier's Boater . . . 55
FRANCE
   Frontière 58
THE NETHERLANDS
   Renaissance Beret 62
GERMANY
   Hunter's Fedora 65

United Kingdom
ENGLAND
   King Edward VI
      Brimmed Beret 68
SCOTLAND
   Glengarry 71
IRELAND
   Cable Braid 74

Scandinavia
FINLAND
Soft Winter Snowflakes 77
LAPLAND
Four Winds Hat 82
Zigs and Zags Stocking Hat . . . 85

North and Central Asia
RUSSIA
Cossack 88
Big Cossack 91
KAZAKHSTAN
Velvet Pillbox 94
AFGHANISTAN
Beaded Cloche 97
Pakul 100
PAKISTAN
Striped Baby Hat 103

Asia
CHINA
Xinjiang Baby Hat 106
Knot-Topped Calotte 109
THAILAND
Folded Bloom 113

JAPAN
Dancer's Hat 117
Samurai Kabuto 121

Abbreviations 128
Glossary and Techniques 129
Sources for Yarns 140
Bibliography 141
Acknowledgments 142
Index 143

HATS ARE MAGICAL. In the twinkling of an eye, a hat can transport you to another place, another state of mind—you can step into a grand adventure through the simple act of putting on a hat. And wearing a hat is not only a means of self-expression, it's an invitation to assume the hat's character and mystique.

Hats are powerful. Reflect on famous people whose headwear signifies their historical importance. Nefertiti, ancient Egypt's most famous queen, is the embodiment of regal beauty. The elegant line of her elongated neck travels upward to her stunning profile to the flat top of her royal *tahj*, an inverted cone headdress. That royal blue crown is an inseparable part of our image of the queen. Likewise, Rembrandt van Rijn, the famous Renaissance artist, cannot be dissociated from his large, softly gathered beret, with which he personifies an elevated aesthetic. The Samurai warrior achieves his fiercest countenance when, after donning all the many layers of his armor, he places the *kabuto* on his head, the final and authoritative statement of his power. And who could imagine Babe Ruth, the most famous player in baseball history, without the telltale crown of his Yankees cap?

Hats precede us. A hat speaks volumes before its wearer utters a word. Casual, relaxed headwear speaks the language of everyday, a wearer completely comfortable with the tasks and focus of daily activities. The hat becomes included as an intimate part of the body, as familiar as face and hands. Conspicuous in their demand for serious attention, hats for formal ceremony or ritual extend the body. Formal hats are generally more complex in creative definition and more spectacular in presentation. They are fashioned with a distinct purpose: to project authority, define status, or designate profession. But in all cases, hats project a quality of character that must be reckoned with.

Hats come in many shapes and sizes, but all spring from one of two categories: a crown with a brim and a crown without a brim. Crowns may be rounded, like the skullcap without a brim or the Panama with a brim, or flat-topped as in a pillbox (thanks to Jackie Kennedy for giving the pillbox its fame). Flat-topped crowns are defined by the structure of their sides and top. Brims may be narrow, they may be wide. Hats may be structured, they may be soft. The rich artistic traditions of cultures from around the world give rise to endless varieties of hats, from very simple to elaborate and complex.

Wander with me in an armchair tour from North America to South America. Sail over to Africa; travel north to Continental Europe and the United Kingdom. Trek farther north into the Scandinavian countries,

turning to cross over the frigid landscape of Russia. Drop down into Central Asia, and complete this winding course in the exotic Far East. I draw from a wealth of visual inspiration displayed in these cultures spanning the globe, letting a motif, a texture, a shape, or a color palette be my springboard into my own interpretation. The thread of continuity in my pursuits is that virtually every country has delightful headcoverings. They are elegant in their simplicity, playful in their whimsy, dramatic in their boldness, and rich in their artistry.

In this book, you'll find a wide range of hat styles, techniques, and sizes. The smallest is the Nigerian baby hat, the largest is the American cowboy hat, the most simple is the Kazakhstan pillbox, the most complex . . . well, you'll have to determine that for yourself. There's plenty of daily wear and ceremonial wonder from which to choose.

I had a glorious time creating this collection for you; I hope you are inspired to make and wear any or all of these hats. Even if you don't think of yourself as a hat person, step outside the (hat)box and give them a whirl. All you need to wear a hat well is a willing head—and a sense of adventure!

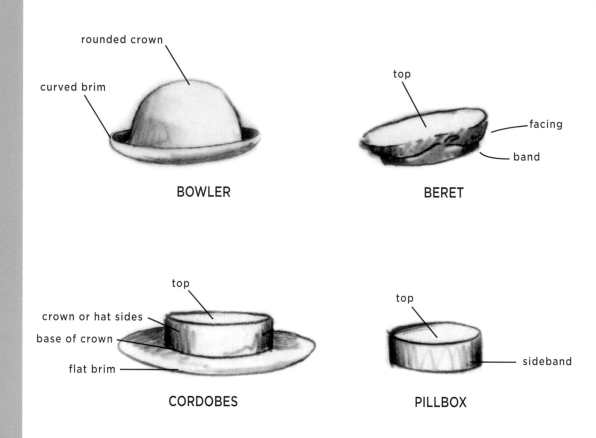

rounded crown

curved brim

BOWLER

top

facing

band

BERET

top

crown or hat sides

base of crown

flat brim

CORDOBES

top

sideband

PILLBOX

ANATOMY OF A HAT

Just as all knitting is made up of two basic stitches (knit and purl), all hats are made up of two basic styles—those with a brim and those without. Beyond that, hat shapes vary widely, but share basic terms to describe similar parts.

The **crown** is the portion of a hat that covers the head—the crown **top** sits at the top of the head; the **base** of the crown is the part that fits around the head.

Crowns may be rounded or structured with defined straight **hat sides,** also called **crown sides** or **sideband,** and a flat **top** (sometimes called a **tip**). The **brim** is the part of the hat that extends away from the crown at the base, and may be found in a wide variety of width and curve options.

TYPES OF HATS

Throughout history, there have been hundreds of hat shapes, and each has been given a specific identifying name. Working to create innovative head coverings, my design collection is a sampling of some common, and many uncommon, types.

A **cloche** has a rounded crown and a very small curved brim (or no brim at all); it is worn down to the eyebrows in front and covers the neck in back.

A **pillbox** has a structured crown, straight hat sides that are perpendicular to a flat top, and no brim; it sits on top of the head.

A **beret** is a relatively unstructured brimless hat with a narrow band that is worn around the circumference of the head. The band merges into the soft sides, then into the flat top.

A Spanish **Cordobes** is a structured shape consisting of straight crown sides, a flat top, and a wide straight brim.

A **fedora** is a higher crowned hat that features a lengthwise crease along the crown, with front "pinch" indentations, and a brim that curves up in the back and slightly down in the front.

A **cowboy hat** has a rounded crown that may be creased in a variety of ways and a brim that slopes away from the base of the crown in a gentle to exaggerated curve. A variety of other silhouettes are included in this book, among them: a deerstalker with earflaps, a close-fitting French hood, and a Cossack with a high-profile crown. Descriptive text and a drawing accompany each pattern.

CLOCHE

PILLBOX

BERET

CORDOBES

FEDORA

COWBOY HAT

MEASURING HEAD CIRCUMFERENCE

To make a hat that fits perfectly, you'll want to measure the head that will wear it. For hats that are to be worn down around the full part of the head (such as a stocking hat, cloche, or skullcap), wrap a cloth tape measure around the fullest part of the head about one inch above the ear (Figure 1).

For hats that are to be worn perched snugly above the full part of the head (such as a Cordobes, cowboy hat, or fedora), wrap the tape measure around the head about two inches above the ear, toward the top of the forehead and slightly above the full part of the back of the head (Figure 2); this measurement ensures that the wearer will have a clear line of sight below the slight dip of the brim.

To measure the crown height for a stocking hat, cloche, or skullcap, pin a ribbon around the head where the hat will be worn, then measure from the bottom edge of the ribbon on one side of the head, up over the top of the head to the bottom edge of the ribbon on the other side (Figure 3). Take a similar measurement from front to back, then average the two measurements to determine the crown height to be knitted.

To determine the crown height on a structured hat (such as a pillbox or fedora), measure straight up (not curved over the head) from the bottom edge of the ribbon to the desired height (Figure 4). Crown heights can vary and are largely determined by personal choice—Dr. Suess's Cat in the Hat likes his crown quite a bit taller than the average three-inch height of a pillbox!

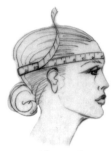

Figure 1

Figure 2

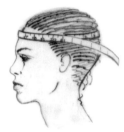

Figure 3

Figure 4

MAKING A SIMPLE HAT FORM

I shaped the more structured hats in this book by hand, sometimes with the help of some household items. However, they may be blocked over hat forms to achieve their characteristic shapes. Commercial hat forms are available online, but you can also make your own. The instructions here are for an inexpensive form that works well for the Gondolier's Boater (page 55), or any hat with a similar crown. Feel free to experiment with this method and sculpt the crown in other rounded contours for a completely custom profile. Let your inner artist guide you.

Purchase four pieces of one-inch-thick Styrofoam circles (available at craft stores) seven inches in diameter. Glue the four circles together, layering one on top of the other (Figure 1), and let them dry. Use a hacksaw or old serrated knife to shave off about half an inch from each side to form an oval block (Figure 2) that is the desired circumference (about 22" for an adult). Shave off the upper edges to round off the top of the block (Figure 3). Use a wood file or coarse sandpaper to smooth the transition from the hat sides to the top. Wrap the finished block with plastic to prevent the Styrofoam from shedding onto the hat and to facilitate slipping the hat on and off the block.

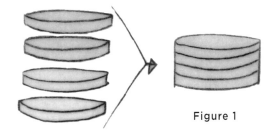

Figure 1

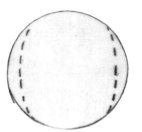

Figure 2

Figure 3

Hat Projects

Deerstalker Hat

H unters of the North American continent sport a practical, yet fun hat called the deerstalker. Whether serious or whimsical, this close-fitting cap with fur-lined brim and ear- and neck flaps is headwear's finest for blocking the wind and cold.

I have designed three options for my knitted hat. The adult size is knitted with bulky yarn and felted a little or a lot for a firm fit, or felted not at all for a soft flexible fit. The child's size is made with worsted-weight yarn and follows the numbers for the adult version. When the child's size is felted, it reduces to a nice compact felt texture. The yarns I have chosen come in a wide range of colors, so feel free to personalize your fashion statement. Here we come, Elmer Fudd!

Deerstalker Hat

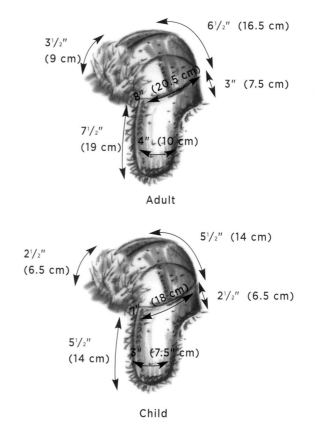

3½" (9 cm)

6½" (16.5 cm)

8" (20.5 cm)

3" (7.5 cm)

7½" (19 cm)

4" (10 cm)

Adult

2½" (6.5 cm)

5½" (14 cm)

7" (18 cm)

2½" (6.5 cm)

5½" (14 cm)

3" (7.5 cm)

Child

The wool outer hat is worked back and forth in rows, starting with a half-circle at one ear. Stitches are picked up along the curved edge of the half-circle, then worked in reverse stockinette stitch to the top of the head. Another piece is made to match and the two pieces are joined along the center top. The brim and earflap sections are knitted downward from the cap. The fur linings are worked separately, then sewn in place.

FINISHED SIZE: **Adult Version A and B:** 23" (58.5 cm) circumference and 6½" (16.5 cm) tall. **Child's Version C:** About 20" (51 cm) circumference and 5½" (14 cm) tall.

YARN: **Versions A and B:** 256 yd (234 m) of chunky (Bulky #5) yarn and 85 yd (78 m) of novelty chunky (Bulky #5) yarn. **Version C:** 220 yd (201 m) of worsted-weight (Medium #4) yarn and 85 yd (78 m) of novelty chunky (Bulky #5) yarn. *We used:* **Felted Adult Version A:** Cascade 128 Tweed (90% Peruvian wool, 10% Donegal tweed; 128 yd [117 m]/100 g): #7602 dark olive, 256 yd (234 m). Crystal Palace Splash (100% polyester; 85 yd [78 m]/100 g) #7181 jaguar, 85 yd (78 m). **Unfelted Adult Version B:** Cascade 128 Tweed (90% Peruvian wool, 10% Donegal tweed; 128 yd [117 m]/ 100 g): #7619 dark charcoal, 256 yd (234 m). Crystal Palace Splash (100% polyester, 85 yd [78 m]/100 g): #7185 sable, 85 yd (78 m). **Child's Version C:** Cascade 220 Tweed (100% wool; 220 yd [201 m]/100 g): #7608 bright pink, 220 yd (201 m). Crystal Palace Splash (100% polyester, 85 yd [78 m]/ 100 g): #7234 carnival, 85 yd (78 m).

NEEDLES: **Version A**—Size 10 (6 mm): 16" (40-cm) circular (cir). **Version B**—Size 9 (5.5 mm): 16" (40-cm) cir. **Version C**—Size 10½ (6.5 mm): 16" (40-cm) cir. **All Versions**—Spare 16" (40-cm) cir needle smaller than size 9 (5.5 mm). **Trim**—Size 10½ (6.5 mm): 16" (40-cm) cir. Adjust needle size if necessary to obtain the correct gauge.

NOTIONS: Tapestry needle; size G/6 (4.25 mm) crochet hook; long sewing pins with colored heads; sharp-point sewing needle and matching thread; beeswax to strengthen sewing thread; two ½" (1.3-cm) snaps (available at fabric store).

GAUGE: **Version A:** 14 sts and 18 rows = 4" (10 cm) in St st with 128 Tweed on size 10 (6 mm) needles; **Version B:** 15 sts and 22 rows = 4" (10 cm) in St st with 128 Tweed on size 9 (5.5 mm) needles, before felting; **Version C:** 14 sts and 18 rows = 4" (10 cm) with 220 Tweed on size 10½ (6.5-mm) needles, before felting.

WOOL OUTER HAT

LEFT SIDE

Half-circle: With needles for gauge and using the long-tail method (see Glossary, page 131), CO 25 sts. Purl 1 (WS) row. *Next row:* (RS) K12, p1, k12. *Next row:* (WS) Purl. Rep the last 2 rows 5 more times—13 rows total. Dec as foll:

Row 1: (RS) K1, ssk, k9, p1, k9, k2tog, k1—23 sts rem.

Row 2: (WS) Purl.

Row 3: K1, ssk, k8, p1, k8, k2tog, k1—21 sts rem.

Row 4: P1, p2tog, p15, ssp (see Glossary, page 133), p1—19 sts rem.

Row 5: K1, ssk, k6, p1, k6, k2tog, k1—17 sts rem.

Row 6: P1, p2tog, p11, ssp, p1—15 sts rem.

Row 7: Sl 1, ssk, psso, BO to last 3 sts, k2tog, BO to end.

Top: With RS facing and beg at lower right corner of half-circle, pick up and knit 42 sts evenly spaced along curved edge, working one-half st in from edge, turn. Cont in rev St st (purl on RS, knit on WS) as foll: Knit 1 row.

Inc row 1: P15, [p1f&b (see Glossary, page 135), p4] 2 times, p1f&b, purl to end—45 sts.

Knit 1 row, purl 1 row, knit 1 row.

Inc row 2: P16, [p1f&b, p5] 2 times, p1f&b, purl to end—48 sts.

Cont even in rev St st until piece measures 2½" (6.5 cm) from pick-up row, ending with a WS (knit) row. Place sts on spare cir needle and set aside.

RIGHT SIDE

Work as for left side, but leave sts on needle.

JOIN LEFT AND RIGHT SIDES

Holding 2 halves of hat tog with WS facing each other, use the three-needle method (see Glossary, page 129) to BO sts tog so that seam is on the RS of the hat. Do not cut yarn. Bring entire ball of yarn through last loop to secure. Beg at center back and using the attached working yarn and crochet hook, work 1 row of single crochet (sc; see Glossary, page 131) around lower edge of hat, easing in any fullness—about 84 sc sts. Fasten off. Weave in loose ends.

BRIM

Measure 3½" (9 cm) out from each side of center front seam (7" [18 cm] total) and mark for brim placement. With RS facing, pick up and knit 25 sts between markers, working in back loops of sc edge. Turn. Cont as foll:

Row 1: (WS) K3, p19, k3.

Row 2: (RS) Knit.

Rep Rows 1 and 2 until piece measures 2½" (6.5 cm) from pick-up, ending with a WS row. Change to garter st (knit every row) and cont as foll: *Dec row:* (RS) K2, ssk, knit to last 4 sts, k2tog, k2—2 sts dec'd. Knit 1 row even. Rep the last 2 rows once more. Rep dec row once more—19 sts rem. With WS facing, BO all sts.

NECK AND EARFLAPS

With RS facing, beg at brim left edge, and working in back loops of sts, pick up and knit 60 sts around lower edge of hat, ending at brim right edge, turn. Cont as foll:

Row 1: (WS) K3, purl to last 3 sts, k3.

Row 2: (RS) Knit.

Rep Rows 1 and 2 until piece measures 2½" (6.5 cm) from pick-up, ending with Row 2 (RS).

Next row: (WS) K3, p9, k36, p9, k3.

Next row: (RS) Knit.

Rep the last 2 rows once more (4 rows total).

Next row: (WS) K3, p9, k6, BO 24 sts (1 st on right needle), k5 (6 sts on right needle), p9, k3—18 sts each side.

Left earflap: Work 18 sts on left side as foll:

Rows 1, 3, 5, and 7: (RS) Knit.

Row 2: (WS) Sl 1 with yarn in front (wyf), bring yarn to back, k1, psso, k4, p9, k3—17 sts rem.

Row 4: Sl 1 wyf, bring yarn to back, k1, psso, k3, p9, k3—16 sts rem.

Row 6: Sl 1 wyf, bring yarn to back, k1, psso, k2, p9, k3—15 sts rem.

Row 8: K3, p9, k3.

*Rep Rows 7 and 8 until flap measures 7" (18 cm) from pick-up row, ending with Row 8 (WS).

Dec row: (RS) K2, ssk, knit to last 4 sts, k2tog, k2—2 sts dec'd.

Next row: (WS) Knit.

Rep the last 2 rows once more. Rep dec row once more—9 sts rem. With WS facing, BO all sts.*

Right earflap: With RS facing, join yarn to right-hand side of rem 18 sts and cont as foll:

Row 1: (RS) Sl 1 wyf, bring yarn to back, k1, psso, knit to end—17 sts rem.

Rows 2, 4, and 6: (WS) K3, p9, knit to end.

Row 3: Sl 1 wyf, bring yarn to back, k1, psso, knit to end—16 sts rem.

Row 5: Sl 1 wyf, bring yarn to back, k1, psso, knit to end—15 sts rem.

Row 7: Knit.

Row 8: K3, p9, k3.

Rep from * to * as described for left earflap.

FINISHING

Button loop on right earflap: With RS facing, insert crochet hook into fourth st of BO edge and draw up loop, ch 5, insert hook into next st and work 1 slip st. Cut yarn, draw tail through last loop to secure, and fasten off. Weave in loose ends.

Felted Adult Version A: Felt according to the instructions on page 134 just enough to fuse the fibers together without reducing the size significantly. As you felt, stop often to check the progress to prevent over felting. Use bath towels to blot out excess water. Invert a mixing bowl of the appropriate circumference over a tall vase to form a blocking stand. (Using a tall vase, or some other tall object as a blocking stand will allow the earflaps to hang free and avoid creases.) Place wet hat over inverted bowl and allow to air dry.

Unfelted Adult Version B: Lightly steam-block earflaps and brim flat.

Child's Version C: Significantly felt hat until sts are nicely compacted. Personalize size by adjusting felting time. Block as for felted adult version.

FUR LINING

ADULT VERSIONS

Fur brim: With size 10½ (6.5 mm) needle, CO 18 sts. Work rev St st (purl on RS, knit on WS) until piece measures 3½" (9 cm) from CO, ending with a WS (knit) row. *Next row:* (RS) P2tog, purl to last 2 sts, p2tog—16 sts rem. With WS facing, BO all sts.

Fur Neck and Earflaps: With size 10½ (6.5 mm) needle, CO 44 sts. Work rev St st until piece measures 3½" (9 cm) from CO, ending with a RS (purl) row. *Next row:* (WS) K12, BO 20 sts, knit to end—12 sts rem for each earflap.

Right earflap: (RS) P10, p2tog—11 sts rem. Cont even in rev St st until piece measures 6½" (16.5 cm) from CO, ending with a purl row. *Next row:* K2tog, knit to last 2 sts, k2tog—9 sts rem. BO all sts.

Left earflap: With RS facing, join yarn to right-hand side of rem 12 sts, p2tog, purl to end—11 sts rem. Cont even in rev St st until piece measures 6½" (16.5 cm) from CO, ending with a RS (purl) row. *Next row:* K2tog, knit to last 2 sts, k2tog—9 sts rem. BO all sts. Weave in loose ends.

CHILD'S VERSION

Fur Brim: With size 10½ (6.5 mm) needle, CO 13 sts. Work rev St st (purl on RS, knit on WS) until piece measures 2½" (6.5 cm) from CO, ending with a WS (knit) row. *Next row:* (RS) P2tog, purl to last 2 sts, p2tog—11 sts rem. With WS facing, BO all sts.

Fur Neck and Earflaps: With size 10½ (6.5 mm) needle, CO 36 sts. Work rev St st until piece measures 2½" (6.5 cm) from CO, ending with a RS (purl) row. *Next row:* (WS) K10, BO 16 sts, knit to end—10 sts rem for each earflap.

Right earflap: (RS) P8, p2tog—9 sts rem. Cont even in rev St st until piece measures 5¼" (13.5 cm) from CO, ending with a purl row. *Next row:* K2tog, knit to last 2 sts, k2tog—7 sts rem. BO all sts.

Left earflap: With RS facing, join yarn to right-hand side next to neck flap, p2tog, purl to end—9 sts rem. Cont even in rev St st until piece measures 5¼" (13.5 cm) from CO, ending with a RS row. *Next row:* K2tog, knit to last 2 sts, k2tog—7 sts rem. BO all sts. Weave in loose ends.

ASSEMBLY

Fold brim up against crown and mark placement of snaps, one close to each corner of brim. Cut a length of sewing thread and draw through a disk of beeswax to coat. "Press" the thread by *quickly* pulling thread under hot iron. With waxed sewing thread and sharp-point needle, sew snaps on crown and knit side of brim. Pin knit side of fur brim to purl side of hat brim, covering seam between crown and brim. With waxed sewing thread and sharp-point needle, use a whipstitch (see Glossary, page 139) to sew in place along the edges. Pin WS of fur flap to purl side of hat, matching center point of fur flap to center of hat flap. Match flap upper corners and ease straight edge of fur along seam line, covering it as before. Pin earflaps for placement, pulling fur slightly around the edges so fur will be seen on RS of hat. Sew button centered onto lower curved edge of left earflap on the wool side. Hat may be worn buttoned with all fur showing on outside, or with flaps hanging down to cover the ears.

Cowboy Hat

There's an old saying about this quintessential icon of the American West: "It's the last thing you take off and the first thing that is noticed." A rugged cowboy with the brim tipped just so against the glare of the setting sun is an indelible popular image.

The son of a Philadelphia master hatter, John B. Stetson designed and created the first cowboy hat in 1865. He created a smooth piece of felt by kneading the underfur collected from a cow hide, dipping it in boiling water, then kneading it and dipping it again. From this piece of felt he made his first hat, and the rest is history, including the name Stetson, which has come to represent a mark of quality, durability, innovation, and beauty.

Cowboy Hat

Although not a Stetson, my felted design honors the American cowboy. There are countless ways to crease the crown and shape the brim, each as individual as the person who wears the hat. Here, I offer two variations for shaping the same knitted pattern. And of course, you will want to care for your hat so it retains its shape. The best place is on your head, next best is in a hatbox that will keep the brim from getting crushed.

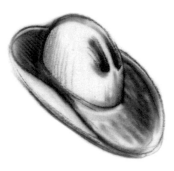

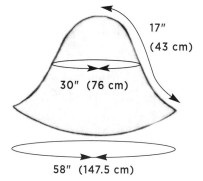

17" (43 cm)

30" (76 cm)

58" (147.5 cm)

This hat is worked in the round from the brim to the top, then felted and shaped.

FINISHED SIZE: About 22 to 23" (56 to 58.5 cm) head circumference. Final measurement is flexible, according to the amount of felting.

YARN: About 250 yd (229 m) of bulky (Bulky #5) yarn. *We used:* Brown Sheep Lamb's Pride Bulky (85% wool, 15% mohair; 125 yd [114 m]/4 oz): 250 yd (229 m). Shown in #M08 wild oak and #M77 blue magic.

NEEDLES: Size 13 (9 mm): 24" (60-cm) and 16" (40-cm) circular (cir) and set of 5 double-pointed (dpn). Adjust needle size if necessary to obtain the correct gauge.

NOTIONS: Marker (m); open-ring marker; tapestry needle; ¾ yd (61 cm) grosgrain ribbon; sharp-point sewing needle and thread to match ribbon; beeswax to strengthen sewing thread; leather belt for hatband.

GAUGE: 10½ sts and 14 rnds = 4" (10 cm) in St st worked in the rnd, before felting (see Glossary, page 134, for working gauge swatches in the rnd).

BRIM

With longer cir needle, CO 150 sts. Place marker (pm) and join for working in the rnd, being careful not to twist sts. Knit 4 rnds—piece should measure 1" (2.5 cm) from CO edge. Shape brim as foll:

Dec rnd 1: *K3, k2tog; rep from *—120 sts rem.
Knit even until piece measures 3½" (9 cm) from CO.
Dec rnd 2: *K4, k2tog; rep from *—100 sts rem.
Knit even until piece measures 6" (15 cm) from CO.
Dec rnd 3: *K3, k2tog; rep from *—80 sts rem.
Place open marker to indicate last rnd of brim.

CROWN

Knit every rnd until piece measures 7" (18 cm) from brim marker. Shape top as foll, changing to shorter cir and dpn when necessary:

Rnd 1: *K6, k2tog; rep from *—70 sts rem.
Rnd 2 and all even-numbered rnds: Knit.
Rnd 3: *K5, k2tog; rep from *—60 sts rem.
Cont in this manner, dec 10 sts every other rnd and working 1 st fewer between decs until 20 sts rem.
Next rnd: *K2tog; rep from *—10 sts rem. Cut yarn, thread tail on a tapestry needle, draw through rem sts, and pull tight to secure. Weave in loose ends.

FINISHING

Felting: Felt according to the instructions on page 134.
Shaping: Firmly pull hat lengthwise from top of crown to brim, being careful not to stretch edge of brim. Place the hat on your head or a rounded bowl of correct circumference. Shape crown to a smooth roundedness. Place hat on flat surface (a countertop or table) and use your palm to hold the base of the crown while pulling the brim away from the crown at a 90-degree angle, defining crown to brim transition, and smoothing brim as you do so. Be careful not to stretch very edge of brim. Brim edges may now be curved up in back and around sides, leaving front of brim flatter, or turned slightly down. Exaggerate the "potato chip" shape of the brim for a distinct western style. Crown indentations may be formed using edge of rigid palm on outside of crown and cupping other hand on the inside of crown to define shape. The tan hat was shaped first with a front-to-back groove in the top of the crown, then indented along the sides. The blue hat was shaped first with the center groove toward the front of the crown, then the side indentations were also squeezed toward the front for an Old West look. Place hat over a tall vase or wide-mouth bottle to keep brim off the countertop or table while it dries.

Attach ribbon: Measure head circumference where you want to wear the hat and cut ribbon 2" (5 cm) longer. Fold one end of ribbon back on itself 1" (2.5 cm). Mark other end of ribbon 1" (2.5 cm) from cut end. Cut a length of sewing thread and draw through a disk of beeswax to coat. "Press" the thread by *quickly* pulling it under a hot iron. With sewing needle and waxed thread, sew folded end along this mark to form a ring. Pin ribbon ring to inside of hat so that lower edge of ribbon aligns with lower edge of crown. Try on hat for fit and adjust ribbon if necessary. With sewing needle and waxed thread, use a whipstitch (see Glossary, page 139) to sew lower edge of ribbon to hat.

Baseball Cap

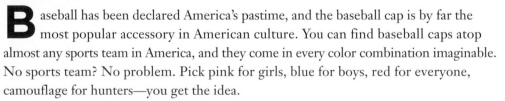

Baseball has been declared America's pastime, and the baseball cap is by far the most popular accessory in American culture. You can find baseball caps atop almost any sports team in America, and they come in every color combination imaginable. No sports team? No problem. Pick pink for girls, blue for boys, red for everyone, camouflage for hunters—you get the idea.

I offer mine in red, white, and blue, the colors of my country. The cotton yarn and thin layer of vinyl-faced foam in the brim make this hat washable, always a key feature when you consider the abuse these hats can take. Wear it brim to the front, brim to the back, brim to the side—there are no rules for sporting this hat!

Baseball Cap

This hat is worked from crown to top. The crown facing is worked in the round, then stitches are worked back and forth in rows, using the intarsia technique (see Glossary, page 137) for the color work. The crown is sewn together along the center back. The brim and its facing are knitted separately, sewn together, then sewn to the lower edge of the crown.

FINISHED SIZE: About 23" (58.5 cm) circumference and 6" (15 cm) tall.

YARN: About 185 yd (169 m) each of three colors of light worsted-weight (Light #3) yarn.
We used: Reynolds Saucy (100% mercerized cotton; 185 yd [169 m]/100 g): #800 white, #361 red, and #251 blue, 185 yd (169 m) each.

NEEDLES: Size 6 (4 mm): 16" (40-cm) circular (cir) and set of 4 double-pointed (dpn). Size 5 (3.75 mm): 16" (40-cm) cir. Adjust needle size if necessary to obtain the correct gauge.

NOTIONS: Marker (m); tapestry needle; ¾ yd (68.5 cm) of 1" (2.5-cm)-wide non-roll elastic; sharp-point sewing needle and white sewing thread; long, straight pins with colored heads; ¼ yd (23 cm) vinyl-faced foam about ⅛" (3 mm) thick for brim (available at fabric stores); ⅝" (1.5 cm) smooth, rounded-face shank button for top of crown.

GAUGE: 20 sts and 26 rows = 4" (10 cm) in St st on larger needle.

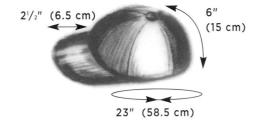

2½" (6.5 cm)   6" (15 cm)

23" (58.5 cm)

CROWN FACING

With white and larger needle, CO 118 sts, leaving a 24" (61-cm) tail for hemming later. Place marker (pm) and join for working in the rnd, being careful not to twist sts. Rnd begins at center back. Work St st (knit every rnd) until piece measures 1¼" (3.2 cm) from CO edge. Change to red and smaller cir needle. Knit 1 rnd, purl 1 rnd (turning ridge). Change to larger cir needle.

CROWN

Foundation rnd: (RS) With red, k1 (selvedge st), *k20 red, k18 white, k20 blue; rep from * once, end k1 blue. Turn work to WS and begin knitting back and forth in rows as foll:

Foundation row: (WS) Keeping colors as established throughout remainder of crown and crossing yarns at color changes to prevent holes, k1 (center back), *p1, k1, purl to last 2 sts of color, k1, p1; rep from * for each color, end k1 in last color.

Row 1: (RS) With red, p1, *sl 1, p1, k16, p1, sl 1; with white, sl 1, p1, k14, p1, sl 1; with blue, sl 1, p1, k16, p1, sl 1; beg with red, rep from * once, end p1 blue. Turn work.

Row 2: (WS) Rep Foundation row.

Rep Rows 1 and 2 until piece measures 2½" (6.5 cm) from turning ridge, ending with a WS row. Dec for top as foll:

Dec row 1: (RS) Matching colors as established, p1 (center back), *sl 1, p1, k2tog, knit to 2 sts before next purl st, ssk, p1, sl 1; rep from * for each color, end p1 blue—12 sts dec'd; 106 sts rem.

Rows 2 and 4: (WS) Work sts as they appear: knit the knit sts; purl the purl sts; purl the slipped sts.

Row 3: (RS) P1 (center back), *sl 1, p1, knit to next purl st, p1, sl 1; rep from * for each color, end p1 blue.

Rep Rows 1–4 two more times—82 sts rem.

Rep Rows 1 and 2 (dec every other row) a total of 3 times—46 sts rem; 6 sts in each white section; 8 sts in each red and blue section, plus 1 selvedge st at each end of row.

Next row: (RS) With red, p1 (center back), *sl 1, p1, k2tog, ssk, p1, sl 1; with white, sl 1, k2tog, ssk, sl 1; with blue, sl 1, p1, k2tog, ssk, p1, sl 1; rep from * for each color, end p1 blue—34 sts rem.

Next row: (WS) Work sts as they appear: knit the knit sts; purl the purl sts; purl the slipped sts.

Next row: (RS) With red, p1, *[ssk] 2 times, k2tog; with white, ssk, k2tog; with blue, [ssk] 2 times, k2tog; rep from * for each color, end p1 blue—18 sts rem.

Cut yarn. Thread blue tail on a tapestry needle, draw through rem sts, and pull tight to secure.

BRIM (make 2; 1 each in blue and white)

Left brim point: With blue, CO 3 sts.

Row 1: (WS) Purl.

Row 2: K1f&b (see Glossary, page 135), knit to end—4 sts.

Row 3: Purl.

Rep Rows 2 and 3 two more times—6 sts. *Next row:* (RS) Using the cable method (see Glossary, page 130), CO 2 sts, knit to end—8 sts. Purl 1 row. Use the cable method to CO 3 sts at beg of next row, knit to end—11 sts. Purl 1 row. Use cable method to CO 4 sts at beg of next row, knit to end—15 sts. Purl 1 row. Use cable method to CO 5 sts, but do not knit the sts in this row. Instead, place all 20 sts on holder, and cut yarn leaving a 6" (15-cm) tail to weave in later.

Right brim point: With blue, CO 3 sts.
Row 1: (WS) Purl.
Row 2: Knit to last st, k1f&b—4 sts.
Row 3: Purl.
Rep Rows 2 and 3 two more times—6 sts. Knit 1 row.
Next row: (WS) Use the cable method to CO 2 sts, purl to end of row—8 sts. Knit 1 row. Use the cable method to CO 3 sts at beg of next row, purl to end of row—11 sts. Knit 1 row. Use the cable method to CO 4 sts at beg of next row, purl to end of row—15 sts.
Join right and left brim points: With RS facing, k15 sts of right brim point, beg at the edge with the 6" (15-cm) yarn tail attached, k20 held left brim point sts—35 sts total. Beg with WS row, work even in St st until piece measures 2¼" (5.5 cm) from last CO row, ending with a WS row. With RS facing and using the sloped method (see Glossary, page 129), BO as foll: BO 2 sts at beg of next 2 rows, then BO 3 sts at beg of next 2 rows, then BO 4 sts at beg of next 2 rows—17 sts rem. BO all sts. With white, work another brim for facing.

FINISHING
With yarn threaded on a tapestry needle, RS facing, and using invisible weaving for reverse stockinette stitch (see Glossary, page 138), sew center back seam.
Blocking: With crown turned WS out, wad up a hand towel for roundness and place inside crown. Lightly steam-block to set sts. Steam-block brim and brim facing flat. Let dry.
Elastic band: Cut elastic to 1" (2.5 cm) longer than head circumference. Form into a ring, overlapping 1" (2.5 cm), and with sewing needle and thread, sew ends tog securely. Place elastic ring inside cap with lower edge of elastic aligned with WS of turning ridge. Fold facing toward WS of cap to enclose elastic. Pin facing in place at color "seams." Thread tapestry needle with long tail left from CO, sew facing to WS of cap, being careful not to pull seaming yarn too tight and cause puckers.
Brim: With WS together, pin brim pieces together around outside edges, leaving inner curved edge open so foam stiffening can be inserted later. With blue, crochet hook, RS facing, and beg at right brim point, work 1 row of single crochet (sc; see Glossary, page 131) around outside curved brim edge. Do not cut yarn. Make a photocopy of brim schematic below and enlarge it so that each square = 1" (2.5 cm) for brim template. Cut vinyl-faced foam to match template. Roll foam, with vinyl facing to outside, lightly around a bottle or a can to encourage curved shape. Slip the foam brim with vinyl toward top into knitted brim from the open edge of the inside curve. Pin these edges together, and work sc around inner curve of brim working 2 sc in each point, completely enclosing the foam brim. With RS tog (this will be blue brim top and cap center front colors red and blue), pin brim to crown, matching center of brim to center front of cap. With blue, use a whipstitch (see Glossary, page 139) to join brim to turning ridge of crown, using every st on turning ridge, and easing sts on inner curve of brim. Lightly steam-block seam from inside of cap to set sts. Sew button onto top of crown.

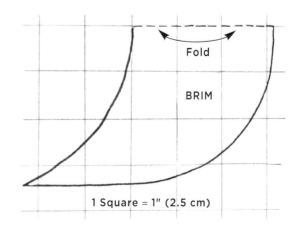

1 Square = 1" (2.5 cm)

Hut Hat

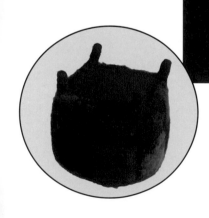

Ancient Andean fiber artists invented many unusual techniques, among which is cut pile, which they used to display colorfully dyed checkerboard and banded patterns of animals, faces, and geometric motifs that are common to all South American knitting designs. I offer a repeat design of a bird in many bright colors for my hut hat, so-called for the four "chimneys" on top. This hat is felted slightly for stability and visual texture. To wear it as Peruvians would, perch it high and forward on your head, but feel free to pull it down like a cloche.

Hut Hat

The hat base is worked back and forth in rows in an ingenious South American knitting technique for working intarsia color patterns that, at the same time, joins every other row into a round, thereby eliminating the need for a seam. The top is worked circularly in rounds.

FINISHED SIZE: About 21" (53.5 cm) circumference and 5" (12.5 cm) tall, excluding "chimneys."

YARN: About 310 yd (284 m) each of five colors of chunky (Bulky #5) yarn.
We used: Baabajoes Wool Pak 14-Ply (100% New Zealand wool; 310 yd [284 m]/250 g): #06 red, #15 blaze, #34 royal blue, #35 aubergine, and #37 royal green, 310 yd (284 m) each (this is enough yarn to make several hats).

NEEDLES: Size 8 (5 mm): 16" (40-cm) circular (cir) and set of 5 double-pointed (dpn). Adjust needle size if necessary to obtain the correct gauge.

NOTIONS: Marker (m); stitch holders or waste yarn; tapestry needle.

GAUGE: 16 sts and 20 rows = 4" (10 cm) in St st, before felting.

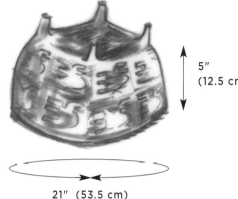

5" (12.5 cm)

21" (53.5 cm)

Knit on RS; purl on WS with colors
as shown on chart.

 #06 red

+ #15 blaze

▲ #34 royal blue

✕ #35 aubergine

◆ #37 royal green

☐ Pattern repeat frame

Hut Hat

Repeat 44 sts within repeat frame two times—88 sts.

BASE

With red and blaze held tog, cir needle, and using the 2-color long-tail method (see Glossary, page 131), CO 88 sts. Do not join into a rnd. Working back and forth in rows, work Rows 1–30 of Hut Hat chart, working color patt in the intarsia method (see Glossary, page 137) joining the seam on knit (RS) rows in the traditional South American technique as foll:

Knit (RS) rows: Knit to the last st in a knit row, slip the last st kwise, use right needle to lift the st in the row below the first st on left needle and place this st on the left needle, then slip the new st to the right needle and work these two sts together as ssk (see Glossary, page 132).

Purl (WS) rows: Keeping in patt, purl all sts.

TOP

With RS facing and red, begin working in rnds. Do not turn work. Knit 1 rnd. *Next rnd:* K3, place marker (pm) to indicate new beg of rnd, place last 6 sts worked onto holder or waste yarn, *k16, place next 6 sts on holder; rep from * 2 more times, k16—64 sts rem. Change to dpn, placing 16 sts from each section onto a separate needle. Dec as foll:

Rnd 1: *Ssk, k12, k2tog; rep from * 3 more times—56 sts rem.

Rnds 2, 4, and 6: Knit.

Rnd 3: *Ssk, k10, k2tog; rep from * 3 more times—48 sts rem.

Rnd 5: *Ssk, k8, k2tog; rep from * 3 more times—40 sts rem.

Rnd 7: *Ssk, k6, k2tog; rep from * 3 more times—32 sts rem.

Beg dec *every* rnd, working 2 sts fewer between ssk and k2tog, until 8 sts rem (2 sts per needle). Cut yarn, thread tail on a tapestry needle, draw through rem sts, and pull tight to secure.

Chimneys: *Place 6 held sts evenly distributed on 3 dpn. Knit 5 rnds even. BO all sts. Cut yarn, thread tail on tapestry needle, and weave in tail on WS of hat. Rep from * for rem 3 chimneys.

FINISHING

Weave in loose ends.

Felting: Follow felting instructions for hand or machine as described on page 134. Felt hat just enough to fuse stitch fibers together, but not so much to shrink circumference more than about 5 percent. Check size often, by trying hat on (it's best to do this on a "bad-hair" day so you won't care that your hair gets wet each time you try the hat on!).

Shaping: Turn hat upside down on a flat surface and press the top with your hands to flatten it. Turn hat right side up and pinch chimneys to stand straight. Roll a bath towel into a cylinder the appropriate size for hat form. Place hat over towel cylinder and let air dry.

Bolivian Derby

The bowler derby commemorates its originator William Bowler, and was popularized by the Earl of Derby. The style found its way to South America, where in Bolivia, Chola women wear this remnant of European influence as part of their daily uniform, and a group of many Chola women working together creates a stunning visual portrait of the culture.

I honor the importance of the llama in South American culture by using a llama-blend yarn, which happens to felt to a beautiful texture. One caution: You must decide how you will wear your hat before you felt it. The length of time felted has determined the fit of each hat shown. The black hat was felted the longest for the most authentic fit, high and forward on the head.

Bolivian Derby

This hat is knitted from side to side with short-row shaping, then felted.

FINISHED SIZE: About 23" (58.5 cm) circumference and 6½" (16.5 cm) tall; brim is about 2" (5 cm) wide and curves upward.

YARN: About 254 yd (232 m) of chunky (Bulky #5) yarn. *We used:* Classic Elite Montera (50% llama, 50% wool; 127 yd [116 m]/100 g): 254 yd (232 m). Shown in #3813 black, #3893 ch'ulla blue, and #3858 cintachi red.

NEEDLES: Size 10.75 (7 mm): straight or 16" (40-cm) circular (cir). Spare needle of same size or 1 or 2 sizes smaller. Adjust needle size if necessary to obtain the correct gauge.

NOTIONS: Open-ring markers (m); tapestry needle; a few yards (meters) smooth cotton waste yarn for provisional CO; size K/10½ (6.5 mm) crochet hook.

GAUGE: 12 sts and 18 rows = 4" (10 cm) in St st, before felting.

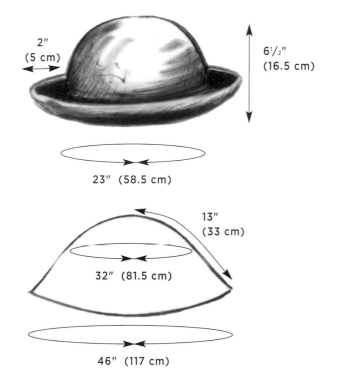

2" (5 cm)

6½" (16.5 cm)

23" (58.5 cm)

13" (33 cm)

32" (81.5 cm)

46" (117 cm)

HAT

Using the crochet chain provisional method (see Glossary, page 130), CO 38 sts. Change to working yarn. Purl 1 row. Knit 1 row. *Purl 1 row. Work short-rows (see Glossary, page 136) as foll:

Short-row 1: (RS) K37, wrap next st, turn.

Short-row 2: (WS) P37.

Short-row 3: K36, wrap next st, turn.

Short-rows 4, 6, 8, 10, 12, and 14: Sl 1, purl to end.

Short-row 5: K34, wrap next st, turn.

Short-row 7: K33, wrap next st, turn.

Short-row 9: K30, wrap next st, turn.

Short-row 11: K13, wrap next st, turn.

Short-row 13: K11, wrap next st, turn.

Short-row 15: K9, wrap next st, turn.

Short-row 16: P9.

Next row: (RS) K38, hiding wraps as you go. Place an open-ring marker at the end of the row to mark end of short-row section.

Rep from * 9 more times—10 short-row sections; working yarn is at center crown. Cut yarn, leaving a 40" (101.5-cm) tail for grafting.

FINISHING

Remove waste yarn from provisional CO and carefully place live sts on spare needle. Thread 40" (101.5-cm) tail on a tapestry needle and use Kitchener st (see Glossary, page 139) to graft live sts tog. Thread a 12" (30.5-cm) length of yarn on tapestry needle and work a running st (see Glossary, page 133) around center crown, weaving in and out of the edge stitches, pull yarn snug to close top of crown hole but not so tight as to prevent felting, and secure.

Felting: Felt according to instructions on page 134 to desired fit—from a gently felted hat that will fit around the head like a cloche to a very firmly felted derby that will sit perched atop the head, or anywhere in between!

Shaping: To shape, you will need a rounded form such as your own head, a bowl of appropriate size, or a purchased hat form. Pull the wet hat firmly down over the form, cuffing the brim in your fingers so as not to stretch the brim edge, and rotate and pull while firmly smoothing the palm of your hand over the surface of the crown. Remove hat from form, and with one hand on the outside of the crown and one on the inside, smooth out any irregularities of shape (you may want to do this over an inverted rounded bowl). Set hat on flat surface and work brim if necessary to encourage a tight upward curve. Let air-dry completely.

Panama Hat

The hat we call a panama is actually made by artisans in Ecuador! Their exquisite workmanship acquired its name in the 1800s when Panama became a center for hat export. Panamas are not worn by the natives, but are a favorite of travelers.

These hats are light and durable, yet soft enough to be rolled into a tube for travel or storage. In Ecuador, fan-shaped palm leaves are gathered, dipped in boiling water, dried, shredded, and bleached with sulphur. The resulting straw is woven into light hats that are perfect sunshields for the face. A bit softer than a traditional panama, my version is still light and comfortable, and it employs a basketweave pattern stitch to emulate woven straw.

Panama Hat

The crown of this hat is worked in the round from the outer crown to the center. The brim is worked separately in the round from crown edge to outer brim edge, then the two pieces are joined with single crochet.

FINISHED SIZE: About 22" (56 cm) circumference and 6" (15 cm) tall; brim is about 3" (7.5 cm) wide.

YARN: About 240 yd (220 m) of worsted-weight (Medium #4) yarn.
We used: Crystal Palace Deco-Ribbon (70% acrylic, 30% nylon; 80 yd [73 m]/50 g): #119 tan, 240 yd (220 m).

NEEDLES: Size 7 (4.5 mm): 16" and 24" (40- and 60-cm) circular (cir) and set of 4 double-pointed (dpn). Adjust needle size if necessary to obtain the correct gauge.

NOTIONS: Marker (m); size F/5 (3.75 mm) crochet hook; tapestry needle.

GAUGE: 20 sts and 22 rnds = 4" (10 cm) in basketweave st worked in the rnd (see Glossary, page 134, for working gauge swatches in the rnd).

STITCH GUIDE

Basketweave Stitch:
(worked in the round)
Rnd 1: Knit.
Rnd 2: Knit into back loop of each st.
Repeat Rnds 1 and 2 for pattern.

Lifted Increase: With right needle tip, lift st below the first st on left needle and place this st on left needle, then knit this lifted st, then knit st on left needle (see Glossary, page 136).

Lifted Increase Through Back Loop:
With right needle tip, lift st below the first st on left needle and place this st on left needle, then knit this lifted st, then knit into the back of the st on the needle to twist it.

22" (56 cm)

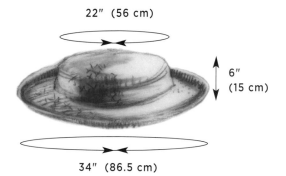

6"
(15 cm)

34" (86.5 cm)

CROWN

With shorter cir needle, CO 112 sts. Place marker (pm) and join for working in the rnd, being careful not to twist sts. Work basketweave st (see Stitch Guide) until piece measures 3¼" (9.5 cm) from beg, ending with Rnd 1 of patt, and dec 2 sts evenly spaced in last row—110 sts rem. Dec as foll (all sts on dec rnds are worked through back loops; all sts on plain rnds are worked as usual), changing to dpn when necessary:

Rnd 1: *K8 through back loops (tbl), k2tog tbl; rep from * 10 more times—99 sts rem.

Rnds 2, 4, 6, 8, 10, 12, and 14: Knit.

Rnd 3: K3 tbl, *k2tog tbl, k7 tbl; rep from * to last 6 sts, k2tog tbl, k4 tbl—88 sts rem.

Rnd 5: K5 tbl, *k2tog tbl, k6 tbl; rep from * to last 3 sts, k2tog tbl, k1 tbl—77 sts rem.

Rnd 7: *K2tog tbl, k5 tbl; rep from * to end of rnd—66 sts rem.

Rnd 9: K2 tbl, *k2tog tbl, k4 tbl; rep from * to last 4 sts, k2tog tbl, k2 tbl—55 sts rem.

Rnd 11: *K3 tbl, k2tog tbl; rep from * to end of rnd—44 sts rem.

Rnd 13: *K2tog tbl, k2 tbl; rep from * to end of rnd—33 sts rem.

Rnd 15: *K1 tbl, k2tog tbl; rep from * to end of rnd—22 sts rem.

Rnd 16: *K1 tbl; rep from * to end of rnd.

Rnd 17: Knit.

Rnd 18: *K2tog tbl; rep from * to end of rnd—11 sts rem. Cut yarn, thread tail on a tapestry needle, draw through rem sts, and pull tight to secure.

BRIM

With smaller cir needle, CO 112 sts. Place marker and join for working in the rnd, being careful not to twist sts. Work basketweave st in the rnd for 4 rnds. Inc as foll:

Rnd 1: *K4, work lifted inc (see Stitch Guide) in next st, k5, work lifted inc in next st; rep from * to last 2 sts, k2—132 sts.

Rnds 2 and 4: *K1 tbl; rep from * to end of rnd.

Rnds 3 and 5: Knit.

Change to longer cir needle. *Note:* The spacing between increases at the end of the next rnd changes slightly to maintain a smooth appearance.

Rnd 6: K1 tbl, work lifted inc tbl (see Stitch Guide) in next st, *k4 tbl, work lifted inc tbl in next st, k5 tbl, work lifted inc tbl in next st; rep from * to last 9 sts, k2 tbl, work lifted inc tbl in next st, k6 tbl—156 sts.

Rnd 7: Knit.

Rnd 8: *K1 tbl; rep from * to end of rnd.

Rnd 9: *K4, work lifted inc in next st; rep from * to last 6 sts, k6—186 sts.

Rnds 10 and 12: *K1 tbl; rep from * to end of rnd.

Rnds 11 and 13: Knit, working jogless join on last st of last plain rnd as foll: knit to last st, sl last st kwise, use right needle to lift st in row below st on left needle onto left needle, then slip it to the right needle, and work these 2 sts as ssk (see Glossary, page 132).

Rnd 14: *K1 tbl, p1; rep from * to end of rnd.

Rnd 15: *P1, k1 tbl; rep from * to end of rnd.

BO all sts loosely while working k1 tbl, p1 rib.

FINISHING

Align CO edges of both pieces with RS tog. With crochet hook, work slip-stitch crochet (see Glossary, page 132), working stitch for stitch to join crown to brim. Weave in loose ends.

Blocking: Spray inside and outside of hat with water. Use the palm of your hand to press and smooth the surface texture of crown and brim. Place hat on a flat surface, such as a countertop, with crown over a biscuit tin of appropriate circumference and height. It will help shape the crown somewhat squarish, but keep the transition soft from hat sides to hat top. Hand-press brim against countertop to define its round shape, and turn outer ½" (1.3 cm) of brim upward. Let air-dry completely.

Raffia Pillbox

African artists use a variety of techniques and materials for fabricating headwear. Some artists make hats with basketry techniques like plaiting and twining. Others shape and sew cloth or leather and skin. Many decorate hats by painting, pyro-engraving, incising, dyeing, or appliquéing and embroidering the base materials.

Raffia is so valuable in the Congo that it's been used as currency. My fiber is a paper "yarn" whose appearance is very close to African raffia. Done in celadon green, this elegant pillbox employs a subtle geometry in the diamond motif and the zigzag of the twisted stitches.

Raffia Pillbox

The twisted rib part of the sideband is worked from bottom to top. The diamond motif is picked up along one short end of the twisted rib and is worked back and forth in rows, then it is sewn to the opposite short end to form a ring. Stitches are picked up from the edge of the ring and worked in the round to the center top.

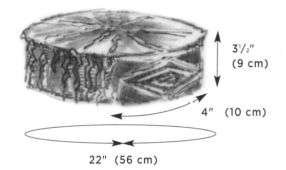

3½" (9 cm)

4" (10 cm)

22" (56 cm)

FINISHED SIZE: About 22" (56 cm) circumference and 3½" (9 cm) tall.

YARN: About 280 yd (236 m) of sport-weight (Fine #2) yarn. *We used:* Habu Textiles Shosenshi Paper (100% linen paper with viscose sizing; 280 yd [256 m]/3 oz[85 g]): celadon green, 280 yd (256 m), used double.

NEEDLES: Size 4 (3.5 mm): 16" (40-cm) cir and set of 4 or 5 double-pointed (dpn). Adjust needle size if necessary to obtain the correct gauge.

NOTIONS: Cable needle (cn); tapestry needle.

GAUGE: 24 sts and 28 rows = 4" (10 cm) in twisted rib st with 2 strands held tog.

STITCH GUIDE

Twisted Rib: (multiple of 3 sts)

Row 1: *Knit into back loop of second st on left needle but leave st on needle, knit first st as usual, slip both sts off needle, p1; rep from * to end of row.

Row 2: *K1, purl into front of second st on left needle but leave st on needle, purl into first st as usual, slip both sts off needle; rep from * to end of row.

Repeat Rows 1 and 2 for pattern.

Knit-twist (K-twist): Knit into back of second st on left needle but leave st on needle, knit first st as usual, slip both sts off needle.

Cable 2 Back (C2B): Sl 1 st onto cn and hold in back, k1, k1 from cn.

CROWN SIDES

With yarn doubled and cir needle, loosely CO 109 sts. Do not join into a rnd. Beg with Row 2, work twisted rib back and forth in rows until piece measures 3½" (9 cm) from beg, ending with a WS row. BO all sts in patt. Do not cut yarn. With RS facing and working yarn still attached, pick up and knit 20 sts along short end of piece just knitted. Knit 1 (WS) row. Work Rows 1–21 of Diamond Cable chart (see page 39). BO all sts kwise. Cut yarn, leaving a 12" (30.5-cm) tail for seaming. To form a cylindrical ring and complete the sides, work as foll: With RS tog, pin the other short end of side piece to BO edge of diamond cable piece. (When worn, the diamond cable section is turned sideways 90 degrees.) With tail threaded on a tapestry needle and using a whipstitch (see Glossary, page 139), sew into a ring, catching BO edge of cable patt and edge st of twisted rib. Turn ring right side out.

CROWN TOP

With working yarn, cir needle, and RS facing, pick up and knit 90 sts evenly spaced around top edge of ring just made. Place marker and join for working in the rnd. *Turning ridge:* Purl 3 rows. Knit 2 rows. *Button st row:* *K1, bring right needle in front of next 2 sts and insert tip between second and third sts on left needle, wrap working yarn around right needle and draw up a loop, slip this loop pwise onto left needle and knit into the back (new st on right needle), slip right needle into the 2 wrapped sts on left needle (these are the first and second sts on left needle) and slip them pwise to right needle, pass new st on right needle over the top of the 2 slipped sts and off needle; rep from *. Knit 2 rnds. Cont as foll:

Rnd 1: *P8, k-twist (see Stitch Guide); rep from * to end of rnd.

Rnd 2: *P8, C2B (see Stitch Guide); rep from * to end of rnd.

Rnd 3: *P6, p2tog, k-twist; rep from * to end of rnd—
81 sts

Rnds 4 and 6: *P7, C2B; rep from * to end of rnd.

Rnd 5: *P7, k-twist; rep from * to end of rnd.

Rnd 7: *P5, p2tog, k-twist; rep from * to end of rnd—
72 sts rem.

Rnds 8 and 10: *P6, C2B; rep from * to end of rnd.

Rnd 9: *P6, k-twist; rep from * to end of rnd.

Rnd 11: *P4, p2tog, k-twist; rep from * to end of rnd—
63 sts rem.

Rnds 12 and 14: *P5, C2B; rep from * to end of rnd.

Rnd 13: *P5, k-twist; rep from * to end of rnd.

Rnd 15: *P3, p2tog, k-twist; rep from * to end of rnd—
54 sts rem.

Rnds 16 and 18: *P4, C2B; rep from * to end of rnd.

Rnd 17: *P4, k-twist; rep from * to end of rnd.

Rnd 19: *P2, p2tog, k-twist; rep from * to end of rnd—
45 sts rem.

Rnd 20: *P3, C2B; rep from * to end of rnd.

Rnd 21: *P1, p2tog, k-twist; rep from * to end of rnd—
36 sts rem.

Rnd 22: *P2, C2B; rep from * to end of rnd.

Rnd 23: *P2tog, k-twist; rep from * to end of rnd—27 sts
rem.

Rnd 24: *P1, C2B; rep from * to end of rnd.

Cut yarn leaving 6" (15-cm) tail, thread tail on a tapestry
needle, draw through rem sts, and pull tight to secure.

FINISHING

To help maintain the pillbox shape, it will be necessary
to prevent the 3 rows of rev St st worked at beg of the
crown top from flattening out when worn. Work as foll:
Turn hat inside out. With doubled yarn threaded on a
tapestry needle, use a whipstitch to seam the top of hat
side where the 90 sts were picked up to the first purl rnd
(as seen from the WS) after the 3 rows of rev St st. Pull

seaming yarn tight to form a rev St st edge on RS of hat.
Seaming this area together creates a stable rev St st
ridge around the hat, and defines the sides and top.
With hat still inside out, lightly steam to block, being
careful not to touch iron to yarn. Turn hat right side
out, and place over a 7" (18-cm) diameter biscuit tin to
shape. (If biscuit tin is too shallow for hat sides, set the
tin on top of a vase or wide-mouth jar.) Steam lightly,
press top down to maintain flat silhouette. Spray sides
with water. Let air-dry.

Diamond Cable

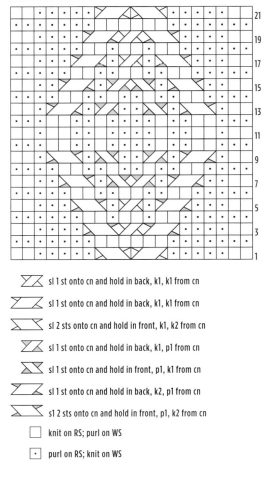

sl 1 st onto cn and hold in back, k1, k1 from cn

sl 1 st onto cn and hold in back, k1, k1 from cn

sl 2 sts onto cn and hold in front, k1, k2 from cn

sl 1 st onto cn and hold in back, k1, p1 from cn

sl 1 st onto cn and hold in front, p1, k1 from cn

sl 1 st onto cn and hold in back, k2, p1 from cn

sl 2 sts onto cn and hold in front, p1, k2 from cn

knit on RS; purl on WS

purl on RS; knit on WS

Gourd Baby Bonnet

Gourds grow in most parts of Africa. Cut and dried, they are used as food bowls, sound boxes for musical instruments, and yes, head coverings. Yellow is the natural gourd color, but it can be dyed with plant dyes after drying. Since pattern and color are important ingredients of everyday African life, carvers often cut a series of geometric shapes into the gourd before it is dyed. Women grow and dry the gourds and are specialists at decorating the surfaces.

A beautifully and intricately carved gourd inspired me to create a baby hat that has an African flavor and yields an interesting process for even the most experienced knitters. The results are spectacular and, most importantly, keep baby comfy and cozy!

Gourd Baby Bonnet

The crown of this hat is worked sideways and shaped with short rows, then grafted into a circle. Stitches for the band are picked up along the outer edge of the crown circle, then worked in the round to the lower edge.

FINISHED SIZE: About 18" (45.5 cm) circumference and 5" (12.5 cm) tall.

YARN: About 114 yd (104 m) each of two colors of sport-weight (Fine #2) yarn.
We used: Dalegarn Svale (50% cotton, 40% viscose, 10% silk; 114 yd [104 m]/50 g): 114 yd (104 m) each of 2 colors.
Bonnet A: #90 black (A) and #9831 gray (B).
Bonnet B: #3108 tangerine (A) and #2005 yellow (B).

NEEDLES: Size 4 (3.5 mm): 16" (40-cm) circular (cir) and set of 4 or 5 double-pointed (dpn). Adjust needle size if necessary to obtain the correct gauge.

NOTIONS: Tapestry needle.

GAUGE: 22 sts and 44 rows = 4" (10 cm) in garter st.

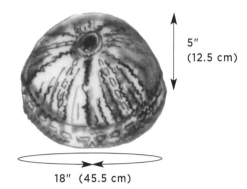

5″
(12.5 cm)

18″ (45.5 cm)

STITCH GUIDE

Button stitch: (worked over 2 sts) *Bring right needle in front of next 2 sts on left needle, insert right needle tip between the second and third sts on left needle, wrap working yarn around right needle and draw up a loop, slip this loop pwise to the left needle tip, and knit into the back of it (1 new st on right needle); slip right needle into the 2 wrapped sts on left needle (the first and second sts on left needle) and slip them pwise to right needle, then pass new st on right needle over the top of the 2 sts slipped sts and off needle; rep from * as directed for each button stitch.

SIDE RING

With A and using the crochet chain provisional method (see Glossary, page 130), CO 20 sts. With A, knit 1 (WS) row. *With B, knit 2 rows. With A, knit 2 rows. Cont in short rows (see Glossary, page 136) as foll (do not hide wraps on rows following short rows):

Short-row 1: (RS) K4 with A, wrap next st, turn work.

Short-rows 2, 4, 6, 8, 10, 12, and 14: (WS) Knit to end using same color as previous row.

Short-row 3: K6 with B, wrap next st, turn work.

Short-row 5: K8 with A, wrap next st, turn work.

Short-row 7: K10 with B, wrap next st, turn work.

Short-row 9: K12 with A, wrap next st, turn work.

Short-row 11: K16 with B, wrap next st, turn work.

Short-row 13: K18 with A, wrap next st, turn work.

Short-row 15: K16 with A, wrap next st, turn work.

Short-row 16: Purl to end. Cut A.

Short-row 17: With B, [k1, work button st] 5 times, wrap next st, turn work. Cut B.

Short-row 18: Attach A, purl to end.

Short-row 19: K18 with A, wrap next st, turn work.

Short-rows 20, 22, 24, 26, 28, and 30: Knit to end, using same color as previous row.

Short-row 21: Attach B, k16, wrap next st, turn work.

Short-row 23: K12 with A, wrap next st, turn work.

Short-row 25: K10 with B, wrap next st, turn work.

Short-row 27: K8 with A, wrap next st, turn work.

Short-row 29: K6 with B, wrap next st, turn work.

Short-row 31: K4 with A, wrap next st, turn work.

Short-row 32: With A, knit to end.

With A, knit 2 rows. Rep from * 4 more times (5 short-row sections), ending the last section with Short-row 32 (i.e., do not knit the last 2 rows with A). Cut A, leaving a tail about 30" (76 cm) long for finishing. Place all sts onto dpn. Remove waste yarn from provisional CO and place 20 live sts onto another dpn. Hold needles parallel with WS of knitting facing tog. Set up sts so the 30" (76-cm) tail is leading from the front needle. Thread tail on a tapestry needle and set up for Kitchener st as foll: insert tapestry needle, insert needle pwise into first st on front needle, and leave this st on needle, insert tapestry needle kwise into first st on back needle and leave this st on needle. Cont according to the Kitchener st (see Glossary, page 139) working Steps 3 and 4 until all sts have been joined. Do not weave in yarn A yet.

CROWN

With B, dpn, and RS facing, pick up and knit 15 sts evenly spaced around top of crown. Place marker (pm) and join for working in the rnd. Purl 1 rnd. Cut B. *Next rnd:* With A still attached, *k1, k2tog; rep from *—10 sts rem. Cut yarn, thread tail on a tapestry needle, draw through rem sts, and pull tight to secure.

FINISHING

With A, cir needle, and RS facing, pick up and knit 99 sts evenly spaced along lower edge of hat. Pm and join for working in the rnd. Purl 1 rnd. Change to B. Knit 1 rnd, purl 1 rnd. Change to A. Knit 1 rnd, purl 1 rnd, knit 1 rnd. *Next rnd:* With B, *k1, work button st; rep from *. Change to A. Knit 1 rnd, purl 1 rnd. Change to B, knit 1 rnd, purl 1 rnd. Change to A. Knit 1 rnd. *Next rnd:* BO all sts pwise. Weave in loose ends. Spray inside of hat with water, place hat over round bowl to shape, spray outside of hat with water. Let air-dry.

Yoruba Bird

The Yoruba tribe of Nigeria regularly transform themselves into compelling art forms. They are best known for spectacular beadwork on their clothing and accessories by which they designate people as warriors, diviners, hunters, musicians, and kings. Tunics, bags, staffs, and most especially elaborate headdresses contribute to these designations.

Yoruba headwear, which can extend one or two feet above the head, often features sculptural human or animal figures. On a ground of indigo blue and sienna brown, I have played bold black geometric shapes for a hat that's more in line with everyday wear. Then whimsy led me to place a bird on top for an ancient affirmation of the king's power.

Yoruba Bird

This hat is worked in the round from the lower crown to center top. The bird is worked separately (shaped with short rows), then sewn to the hat top.

FINISHED SIZE: About 22" (56 cm) circumference and 7½" (19 cm) tall.

YARN: About 191 yd (175 m) each of three colors of DK-weight (Light #3) yarn.
We used: Cascade Sierra (80% pima cotton, 20% wool; 191 yd [175 m]/100 g): #02 black, #21 blue, and #59 sienna, 191 yd (175 m) each.

NEEDLES: Size 5 (3.75 mm): 16" (40-cm) circular (cir) and set of 4 or 5 double-pointed (dpn). Adjust needle size if necessary to obtain the correct gauge.

NOTIONS: Marker (m); removable marker or safety pin; tapestry needle; small amount of polyester fiberfill or a few cotton balls for stuffing.

GAUGE: 21 sts and 28 rnds = 4" (10 cm) in St st worked in the rnd (see Glossary, page 134, for working gauge swatches in the rnd).

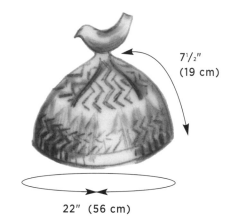

7½" (19 cm)

22" (56 cm)

BRIM

With black and cir needle, CO 118 sts. Place marker (pm) and join for working in the rnd, being careful not to twist sts. Join blue and work 2-color rib as foll: *K1 black, p1 blue; rep from * to end of rnd. Work 4 more rnds in 2-color rib as established. Work Rnd 1 of Lower Hat chart (see page 46), dec 2 sts evenly spaced—116 sts rem. Work Rnds 2–10 of chart. *Next rnd:* With blue, knit, dec 2 sts evenly spaced—114 sts rem. Work Rnds 1–6 of Upper Hat chart. *Next rnd:* With sienna, knit, dec 2 sts evenly spaced—112 sts rem.

CROWN

Work Rnds 1–24 of Crown chart—12 sts rem. Work even in colors as established until piece measures ¾" (2 cm) from end of chart. With black, BO all sts. Cut yarn, leaving a 12" (30.5-cm) tail to attach bird to top of crown.

FINISHING

Weave in loose ends. Spray with water inside and out, and set over inverted bowl of correct size to block to shape. Let air-dry completely.

BIRD

Tail: With blue and dpn, CO 12 sts, leaving a 12" (30.5-cm) tail for seaming. Divide sts evenly on 3 dpn (4 sts each needle) and join, being careful not to twist sts. Knit 4 rnds—piece should measure about ¾" (2 cm) from beg. *Dec rnd:* K1, [k2tog, k2] 2 times, k2tog, k1—9 sts rem (3 sts on each needle). Knit 4 rnds—piece should measure about 1¼" (3.2 cm) from beg.

Belly: Inc as foll:

Rnd 1: Needle 1: k3 for back of bird, placing removable marker in second of these sts; needle 2: k1, work lifted inc (see Glossary, page 135) in next st, k1; needle 3: k1, lifted inc in next st, k1—11 sts.

Rnd 2: K3, [lifted inc in next st, k2, lifted inc in next st] 2 times—15 sts.

Rnd 3: Knit.

Rnd 4: K3, k1, [lifted inc in next st, k2] 3 times, lifted inc in next st, k1—19 sts.

Rnd 5: K6, lifted inc in next st, k8, lifted inc in next st, k3—21 sts.

Rnd 6: Knit.

Work short rows (see Glossary, page 136) as foll:

*Short-row 1: Wrap first st by slipping first st purlwise to right needle, bring yarn forward, slip st back to left needle, bring yarn to back, turn work.

Short-row 2: P18, wrap next st by slipping st to right needle, take yarn to back, slip st back to left needle, yarn forward, turn work.

Short-row 3: K18 to end of rnd.

Knit 1 rnd, hiding wraps by working wraps tog with wrapped sts. If necessary, reposition 1 st each side of marked st so there are 3 sts on needle 1 for the bird's back. Rep from * once more.

Short-row 7: Sl first st to right needle, wrap this st and return it to left needle, turn.

Short-row 8: P1, p2tog, p12, p2tog, p1, wrap next st, turn.

Short-row 9: K16 to end of rnd, turn.

Short-row 10: K16, hiding wraps as before, wrap next st, turn.

Short-row 11: P10, wrap next st, turn.

Short-row 12: Knit 13 to end, hiding wraps as needed.

Next rnd: K3, [k2tog] 8 times (a wrap will need to be picked up and knit with the second k2tog)—11 sts rem.

Short-row 13: Sl first st to right needle, wrap this st and return it to left needle, turn work; p8, wrap next st, turn.

Short-row 14: K8 to end of rnd.

Next rnd: Knit 1 rnd, hiding wraps as before.

Knit 3 rnds even.

Knit on RS in colors as shown.

■ #02 black

▣ #21 blue

◈ #59 sienna

◬ Vertical double decrease in black: sl 2tog kwise, k1, p2sso

☐ No stitch

▢ Pattern repeat

Upper Hat

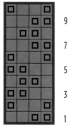

Work 5-st rep 19 times—114 sts.

Lower Hat

Work 4-st rep 29 times, dec 2 sts evenly spaced on first rnd—116 sts.

Crown

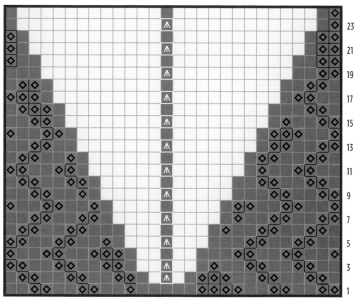

Work stitch patt 4 times.

Head: Cont as foll:

Rnd 1: Work lifted inc in first st, k1, lifted inc in next st, k2, [k2tog] 2 times, k2—11 sts.

Rnd 2: Knit.

Rnd 3: [Lifted inc in next st, k1] 2 times, lifted inc in next st, knit to end—14 sts.

Rnd 4: K9, [k2tog] 2 times, k1—12 sts rem.

Rnd 5: [K2tog] 4 times, knit to end—8 sts rem.

Rnd 6: K4, [k2tog] 2 times—6 sts rem.

Rnd 7: [K2tog] 3 times—3 sts rem.

Cut yarn, leaving a 12" (30.5-cm) tail. Thread tail on a tapestry needle, draw through rem sts, and pull tight to secure. Insert needle into beak tip and back out of bird about 3 rows before the tip. Tightly wrap yarn around beak to form a point, then secure yarn tail by *working a backstitch (see Glossary, page 138) around the running strand between 2 sts; rep from * once more between 2 other sts. Then embed the yarn tail into the bird to hide.

FINISHING

Stuff bird with fiberfill (or fluffed cotton balls), shaping it into a uniform, round form. Thread CO tail onto a tapestry needle and use a whipstitch (see Glossary, page 139) to close the tail vertically. Backstitch around a running strand between 2 sts to secure yarn tail and hide same as before. With black threaded on tapestry needle, whipstitch bird to top of hat. Weave in loose ends.

Ruffled Dignity

Throughout the Cameroon Grassfields, headwear and other forms of dress convert material wealth into symbolic prestige. On formal occasions, a Grassfields man wears a distinctive hat to assert his ethnic identity, allude to Grassfields history and cultural values, and to underscore his social status and his sphere of influence within the community.

Texture is the key, as in so many African artistic endeavors. Actual texture in the linen yarn resembles raffia, the natural African palm fiber used in garment and accessory making most widely seen in central Africa. Visual texture figures in the ruffle at the top edge of the extended pillbox shape. Worn with sides extended, the hat has a regal air; worn with sides folded up, the hat becomes casual. Either way, the wearer will command attention for the unusual.

Ruffled Dignity

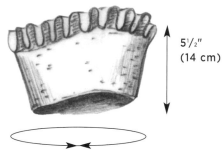

5½"
(14 cm)

21½" (54.5 cm)

This hat begins with the crochet ruffle, which is worked into a ring. Stitches for the sides are picked up from the ring and knitted downward in the round. Stitches for the crown top are then picked up from the other edge of the ring and worked in the round to the center of the crown top.

FINISHED SIZE: About 21½" (54.5 cm) circumference and 5½" (14 cm) tall.

YARN: About 300 yd (274 m) of worsted-weight (Medium #4) yarn.
We used: Euroflax Heathers Chunky (100% linen, 150 yd [137 m]/100 g): #16.2852 Oriental grass, 300 yd (274 m).

NEEDLES: Size 7 (4.5 mm): 16" (40-cm) circular (cir) and set of 4 or 5 double-pointed (dpn). Adjust needle size if necessary to obtain the correct gauge.

NOTIONS: Marker (m); tapestry needle; size G/6 (4.25 mm) crochet hook.

GAUGE: 20 sts and 36 rnds = 4" (10 cm) in linen st on size 7 (4.5 mm) needles (see Glossary, page 134, for working gauge swatches in the rnd). Crochet gauge: 10 ladder rungs with 7 dc ruffle on each rung (see Stitch Guide at right; see Glossary, page 131–132, for crochet instructions) = 4" (10 cm).

STITCH GUIDE

See Glossary, pages 131–132 for crochet instructions.

To test crochet gauge: Work ladder rungs as foll (*Note:* [Tc, ch 1, skip 1] counts as 1 ladder rung and the space between rungs):
Foundation ch: Ch 21.
Foundation ladder: Tc in 4th ch from hook, *ch 1, skip 1 ch, tc in next ch; rep from * to last ch in foundation.
Begin ruffles: Ch 2, work 7 dc over first rung of ladder working from right to left across the tc rung, 1 dc over ch-1 from foundation ch between first and second rungs, rotate the work so the next set of 7 dc can continue across the next rung from right to left. Do not allow the foundation ladder to become twisted. The rungs should be clearly visible on the WS of the work; all the ruffles are on the RS of the work.
Second rung: (work right to left across rung) Work 7 dc over second rung, work 1 dc over ch-1 between second and third rungs. Rotate work.

Third rung: (work right to left across rung) Work 7 dc over third rung, work 1 dc over ch-1 between third and fourth rungs. Rotate work.
Cont each rung of the foundation ladder as foll: *Work 7 dc over next rung, 1 dc over ch-1 from foundation ch between next 2 rungs, rotate work; rep from * to end of foundation ladder.

Linen Stitch: (multiple of 2 +1 sts)
Rnd 1: *K1, bring yarn to front, sl 1 pwise, bring yarn to back; rep from * to end of rnd, end last rep k1.
Rnd 2: *Bring yarn to front, sl 1 pwise, bring yarn to back, k1; rep from * to end of rnd, end last rep sl 1 pwise.
Repeat Rnds 1 and 2 for pattern.

Double Decrease: (3 sts decreased to 1 st) If the first st to be worked in the double decrease is a knit st, work k3tog; if the first st to be worked in the double decrease is a slip st, work p3tog.

CROCHET RUFFLE

Foundation ch: With crochet hook, ch 97 sts for foundation, then ch 3 more (counts as 1 rung of ladder).

Foundation ladder: Work tc in fourth ch from hook, *ch 1, skip 1 ch, tc in next ch; rep from * to end of foundation ch—50 rungs in ladder.

First rung: Ch 2, work 7 dc over first rung of ladder (working across rung from right to left), 1 dc over ch-1 between first and second rungs, rotate work to be able to cont to crochet across the next rung from right to left.

Second rung: Work 7 dc over second rung, work 1 dc over ch-1 between second and third rungs. Rotate work.

Third rung: (work across the rung from right to left) Work 7 dc over third rung, work 1 dc over ch-1 between third and fourth rungs. Rotate work.

Cont to work 7 dc over each rung and 1 dc over ch-1 between next 2 rungs to end of foundation ladder. Do not allow foundation ladder to become twisted. Cut yarn, draw tail through last loop, and pull tight to secure. Join foundation ladder into a ring as foll: Thread tail on tapestry needle and insert through last dc and into the foundation ladder, hold first and last ruffles together and whipstitch (see Glossary, page 139) tog across bottom edges of first dc made on first rung, and last dc worked on last rung to secure.

HAT SIDES

Join yarn and sc 109 sts evenly along one lengthwise edge of foundation ladder. Cut yarn, draw tail through rem loop, and pull tight to secure. Fasten off.

Join for knitting: With cir needle and RS facing, pick up and knit 1 st in back loop of each sc along foundation ladder—109 sts. Place marker and join for working in the rnd. Work linen st in the rnd (see Stitch Guide) for 4" (10 cm). BO all sts while working k1, p1 rib (knit the slipped sts and purl the knit sts of the previous rnd).

CROWN TOP

Sc 109 sts evenly along other lengthwise edge of foundation ladder. Cut yarn, draw tail through last loop, and pull tight to secure. Fasten off.

Join for knitting: With cir needle and RS facing, pick up and knit 1 st in back loop of each sc along the foundation ladder—109 sts. Place marker and join for working in the rnd. Work linen st for 2 rnds. *Next rnd:* [Work 22 sts, pm] 4 times, work last 21 sts to end of rnd (the last section has 1 st fewer than the other 4 sections). *Dec rnd:* Cont in linen st, [work to 3 sts before marker, work double dec (see Stitch Guide)] 5 times—10 sts dec'd. Work 2 rnds even. Rep the last 3 rnds from * 8 more times, changing to dpn when necessary—19 sts rem. *Next rnd:* [P2tog] 8 times, p3tog—9 sts rem. Cut yarn, draw tail through rem loops, and pull tight to secure. Fasten off. Weave in loose ends.

FINISHING

Steam-block lightly as foll: turn hat inside out and lay crown, as flat as possible, over the end of an ironing board. Lightly touch iron to back of work, being careful not to crush crocheted edge. Turn hat right side out and lightly touch iron to inside of hat sides. Rotate hat to steam entire cylinder. Spray ruffle with water. Lay hat upside down and arrange so that top is flat and sides stand up by themselves. Let air-dry completely.

Cordobes with Scarf

From Cordova in the Andalusian region of southern Spain, come the famous wide, flat-crowned, straight-brimmed Cordobes hats. Sometimes called boleros after the Spanish dance, the hats are popular with all Andalusian men and women, and they're almost always black or red. In a country profuse with lavish and dramatic clothing, from the extravagant tiered colorful dresses of the women to the tightly fitted waist-length jackets, ruffled shirts, and full-length trousers of the men, the Cordobes emerges as the most recognizable symbol of mannered elegance that is wholly Spanish.

The llama/wool yarn I have chosen felts to a beautiful, supple surface texture with enough stability to maintain its shape. I have embellished this unique silhouette with a stylish attached scarf so you can wrap yourself in my interpretation of this Spanish tradition.

Cordobes with Scarf

This hat is worked in the round from brim to top, then felted and shaped. The scarf is worked separately and sewn to the base of the crown.

FINISHED SIZE: About 22" (56 cm) circumference and 2½ to 3" (6.5 to 7.5 cm) tall; brim is about 2½" (6.5 cm) wide.

YARN: Hat: About 254 yd (232 m) of bulky (Bulky #5) yarn. **Scarf:** About 246 yd (225 m) of worsted-weight (Medium #4) yarn.
We used: **Hat:** Classic Elite Montera (50% llama, 50%wool; 127 yd [116 m]/100 g): #3813 black, 254 yd (232 m). **Scarf:** Classic Elite Lush (50% angora, 50% wool; 123 yd [112 m]/50 g): #4413 black, 246 yd (225 m).

NEEDLES: Hat—Size 10½" (6.5 mm): 24" (60-cm) circular (cir) and set of 4 or 5 double-pointed (dpn). Scarf—Size 9 (5.5 mm): 24" (60-cm) cir. Adjust needle size if necessary to obtain the correct gauge.

NOTIONS: Markers (m); tapestry needle; long sewing pins; sewing thread; beeswax for strengthening thread; sharp-point sewing needle; safety or coilless pin.

GAUGE: 20 sts and 24 rnds = 5¾" (14.5 cm) with Montera worked in St st on larger needles, before felting; 15 sts and 18 rows = 4" (10 cm) in Lush worked in St st on smaller needles.

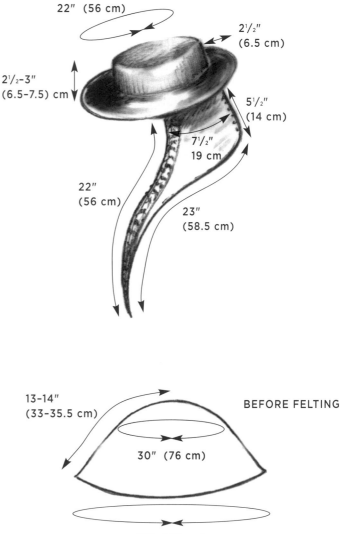

22" (56 cm)

2½" (6.5 cm)

2½-3" (6.5-7.5) cm

5½" (14 cm)

7½" 19 cm

22" (56 cm)

23" (58.5 cm)

13-14" (33-35.5 cm)

BEFORE FELTING

30" (76 cm)

48" (122 cm)

HAT

BRIM

With Montera and larger needles, CO 171 sts. Place marker (pm), and join for working in the rnd, being careful not to twist sts. Knit 2 rnds. Cont as foll:

Rnd 1: [K17, k2tog] 9 times—162 sts rem.

Rnd 2 and all even-numbered rnds: Knit.

Rnd 3: [K16, k2tog] 9 times—153 sts rem.

Rnd 5: [K15, ssk] 9 times—144 sts rem.

Rnd 7: [K14, k2tog] 9 times—135 sts rem.

Rnd 9: [K13, ssk] 9 times—126 sts rem.

Rnd 11: [K12, k2tog] 9 times—117 sts rem.

Rnd 13: [K11, ssk] 9 times—108 sts rem.

Rnd 15: [K10, k2tog] 9 times—99 sts rem.

Knit even until piece measures about 4¼" (11 cm) from last dec.

CROWN

Rnd 1: [K9, k2tog] 9 times—90 sts rem.

Rnd 2 and all even-numbered rnds: Knit.

Rnd 3: [K8, k2tog] 9 times—81 sts rem.

Rnd 5: [K7, k2tog] 9 times—72 sts rem.

Cont to dec in this manner, working 1 st fewer between decs until 18 sts rem (last rnd will be [k1, k2tog]). *Next rnd:* [K2tog] 9 times—9 sts rem. Cut yarn, draw tail through rem sts, and pull tight to secure. Fasten off. Weave in all ends.

FINISHING

Felting: Felt according to instructions on page 134 until when folded flat, hat measures 11" (28 cm) at base of crown. Rinse thoroughly and blot out excess water with bath towels.

Shaping: Hold top of crown and pull brim downward to smooth lengthwise grain of knitting, working around entire brim. Shape hat over a form (I used a lidded biscuit tin that measures 7" [18 cm] in diameter and 2¾" [7 cm] tall). Place tin or form on countertop or other flat surface. Place crown of hat on form and, with palm of hand, smooth top of hat flat. Make a sharp crease at top-to-side "corner," and smooth hat sides to base of crown where bottom of form meets countertop. Firmly press brim flat onto countertop, pulling slightly on brim where needed to shape evenly round. Let air-dry completely.

SCARF

With Lush and smaller needles, CO 57 sts. (*Note:* To provide contrast with the St st background, the lace insert patt is worked with purl sts on the RS of the work, and the knit sts on the WS.)

Row 1: (WS) *K1, p1, yo, sl 1, k1, psso, k1, sl 1, k1, psso, yo, p1, k1*, place marker (pm), purl to last 9 sts, pm, rep from * to * once.

Row 2: (RS) *K2, p5, k2*, slip m (sl m), knit to last 9 sts, sl m, rep from * to * once.

Row 3: *K1, p1, k1, yo, sl 1, k2tog, psso, yo, k1, p1, k1*, sl m, purl to last 9 sts, sl m, rep from * to * once.

Mark the center st with a safety or coilless pin before starting next row. Move pin upward every 4th row to identify marked center st.

Row 4: K2, p5, k2, sl m, knit to center st, yo, k1 (center st), yo, knit to marker before last 9 sts, sl m, k2, p5, k2—59 sts.

Rep these 4 rows 5 more times. Then work Rows 1–3 once more—69 sts. Place m each side of center 11 sts.

Next row: (Row 4 of patt) Work 29 sts in patt to marked 11 sts, place these 29 sts on holder, BO next 11 sts, work in patt to end—29 sts each side. Remove m each side of 11 BO sts and remove pin from center st; retain m in place at each side edge lace inserts. *Note:* To produce a smooth bind-off edge, use the sloped method (see Glossary, page 129) for subsequent bind-offs.

SHAPE SCARF TIE

Right tie (as hat is worn): Work as foll:

Row 1: (WS) K1, p1, yo, sl 1, k1, psso, k1, sl 1, k1, psso, yo, p1, k1, sl m, purl to last st (1 st unworked on left needle), turn work to RS—29 sts.

Row 2: (RS) Beg at center back, sl 1 from left to right needle (2 sts on right needle), BO 1 st, k1, BO 1, k1, BO 1, knit to m, k2, p5, k2—26 sts rem.

Row 3: K1, p1, k1, yo, sl 1, k2tog, psso, yo, k1, p1, k1, sl m, purl to last st (1 st on left needle), turn work to RS.

Row 4: Sl 1 from left to right needle, BO 1 st, k1, BO 1, knit to m, k2, p5, k2—24 sts rem.

Row 5: Rep Row 1.

Rows 6 and 8: Rep Row 4—20 sts rem after Row 8.

Row 7: Rep Row 3.

Row 9: K1, p1, yo, sl 1, k1, psso, k1, sl 1, k1, psso, yo, p1, k1, sl m, purl to end of row.

Row 10: Ssk, knit to m, k2, p5, k2—19 sts rem.

Row 11: K1, p1, k1, yo, sl 1, k2tog, psso, yo, k1, p1, k1, sl m, purl to end of row.

Row 12: Knit to m, k2, p5, k2.

Row 13: K1, p1, yo, sl 1, k1, psso, k1, sl 1, k1, psso, yo, p1, k1, sl m, purl to end of row.

Rep Rows 10–13 until 2 sts rem. When there are too few to complete the 9-st lace patt at the beg of WS and end of RS rows, work these sts in garter st, while maintaining the first 2 sts on RS rows and last 2 sts on WS rows in patt. BO all sts. Cut yarn, leaving 4" (10-cm) tail and pull tail through rem st to secure.

Left tie: With WS facing, join yarn at center back. Work as foll:

Row 1: (WS) Beg at center back, sl 1, p1, BO 1 st purlwise, p1, BO 1 purlwise, p1, BO 1 purlwise, purl to m, k1, p1, yo, sl 1, k1, psso, k1, sl 1, k1, psso, yo, p1, k1—26 sts rem.

Rows 2, 4, and 6: (RS) K2, p5, k2, sl m, knit to last st (1 st unworked), turn work to WS.

Rows 3 and 7: (1 st on right needle from previous row) Sl 1 from left needle, BO 1 purlwise, p1, BO 1 purlwise, purl to m, k1, p1, k1, yo, sl 1, k2tog, psso, yo, k1, p1, k1—2 sts dec'd.

Row 5: (1 st on right needle from previous row) Sl 1, BO 1 purlwise, p1, BO 1 purlwise, purl to m, k1, p1, yo, sl 1, k1, psso, k1, sl 1, k1, psso, yo, p1, k1—22 sts rem.

Row 8: K2, p5, k2, sl m, knit to end of row.

Row 9: Ssp (see Glossary, page 133), purl to m, k1, p1, yo, sl 1, k1, psso, k1, sl 1, k1, psso, yo, p1, k1—19 sts rem.

Row 10: K2, p5, k2, knit to end of row.

Row 11: Purl to m, k1, p1, k1, yo, sl 1, k2tog, psso, yo, k1, p1, k1.

Row 12: K2, p5, k2, knit to end of row.

Rep Rows 9–12 until 2 sts rem. Change to garter st when there are too few sts to work lace patt, while maintaining first 2 sts of RS rows and last 2 sts of WS rows in patt. BO and finish as for right tie.

Edging: With Lush and RS facing, pick up and knit about 140 sts evenly spaced along St st curved edge of scarf. With WS facing, BO all sts kwise.

FINISHING

Weave in loose ends. Steam or wet-block scarf. Pin straight edge of scarf to back half of hat at base of crown on inside, matching center back RS (knit side) of scarf to center back WS of hat. Cut a length of sewing thread and draw through a disk of beeswax to coat. "Press" the thread by *quickly* pulling it under a hot iron. With sewing needle and waxed thread, whipstitch (see Glossary, page 139) scarf to hat.

Gondolier's Boater

As an enduring symbol of the romance of Venice, gondoliers stand second to none. It used to be that gondoliers had to be Venetian by birth, and the job passed down from father to son. A special course and exam covering everything from the history of architecture to singing were required before the gondolier had the right to wear his identifying straw hat.

My choice of linen softens the straw hat's look. After making a gazillion inches (this is a distinct exaggeration) of knitted cord, you shape the hat by coiling the cord over a hat form and sewing the concentric ovals together. You work from the top of the crown down and define the shape of the brim and keep it firm with the final knitted cord oval. To look like a real Venetian gondolier, tie a ribbon around the base of the crown.

Gondolier's Boater

This hat is constructed from a long strip of knitted cord (I-cord) that is coiled around itself from the center of the crown downward to the brim, and sewn in place.

FINISHED SIZE: About 22" (56 cm) circumference and 4" (10 cm) tall; brim is about 3" (7.5 cm) wide.

YARN: About 600 yd (549 m) of worsted-weight (Medium #4) yarn.
We used: Euroflax Heathers Chunky (100% linen; 150 yd [137 m]/100 g): #16.2872 chamomile, 600 yd (549 m).

NEEDLES: Size 7 (4.5 mm): set of 2 double-pointed (dpn). Adjust needle size if necessary to obtain the correct gauge.

NOTIONS: Tapestry needle; long sewing pins with colored heads; safety or coilless pin; hat form (see page 11 for making a hat form).

GAUGE: 16 rows of 3-st knitted cord measures about ⅜" (1 cm) wide and 4" (10 cm) long.

22" (56 cm)

3" (7.5 cm)

4" (10 cm)

I-CORD STRIP

CO 3 sts. Work 3-st knitted cord (see Glossary, page 137) until piece measures about 50 feet (15.25 meters). Place sts on safety or coilless pin (so you can adjust the final length during assembly).

ASSEMBLY

Crown: Measure 2" (5 cm) from CO edge of knitted cord and fold back to lay parallel to next 2" (5 cm) of cord. Lay on flat surface and coil cord around itself to create an oval, being careful to keep the cord untwisted. *Work 3 or 4 concentric rings, then insert pins from the outer edge toward the center to hold the rings in place. Thread about 24" (61 cm) of yarn on a tapestry needle, and with WS facing and working from the outer edge toward the center, insert threaded needle into the cord from the outer edge of the oval toward the center, then back to the outer edge as shown at right. Rep from * until piece measures about 6" (15 cm) wide and 7" (18 cm) long, rethreading needle as necessary. Steam-press lightly to flatten. Lay piece on top of hat form and continue to coil cord around itself, rounding the crown shape and working down to the inner edge of brim, and sewing 3 to 4 concentric rings at a time, until entire hat form is covered.

Brim: Continue to coil cord against flat surface, sewing 3 to 4 concentric rings at a time until brim measures 3" (7.5 cm), but do not sew the last row. Add or subtract a few rows of cord, if necessary. Place hat (still on hat form) on ironing board and steam press brim, keeping last coil length free. Let air-dry. Add one more coil on top of previous coil to make a rim on the brim, working this coil a bit tighter so that brim will turn up slightly and maintain its shape. On last row of cord, work sl 1, k2tog, psso—1 st rem. Cut yarn, leaving a 4" (10-cm) tail, and draw tail through last st. Thread tapestry needle with rem tail and weave into center of cord to secure. For the authentic look of a Gondolier, tie a black ribbon around the base of the crown.

ASSEMBLY

Sew knitted cord into a spiral by inserting sewing needle from outer edge towards center and back out to outer edge.

Frontière

When she went to France to marry Henry II in the sixteenth century, Catherine de Medici wore a version of the French hood, popular at the time all over Europe. The French hood was a stiff open cap shaped like a "C" that was worn with the points curving around the chin. When Catherine became a widow, she added a dip over the forehead, the source of the term "widow's peak," and the headdress became known as a frontière. In the 1500s, frontières were made of black velvet or a rich satin or taffeta brocade with decorative jeweled and pearled edges.

My close-fitting cap of cotton chenille offers a surface texture similar to cut velvet. The French knots are a knitter's version of the pearled edges. All in white, the frontière would be fit for a bride.

Frontière

This hat is worked in rows from the black border at the front, across the top of the head, then to the lower back, and is shaped with increases and decreases along the way.

FINISHED SIZE: About 22" (56 cm) circumference (will stretch to 24" [61 cm]).

YARN: About 98 yd (90 m) each of three colors of sport-weight (Fine #2) yarn (used doubled).
We used: Crystal Palace Cotton Chenille (100% cotton; 98 yd [90 m]/50 g): #9598 black, #6246 blue, and #1058 white, 98 yd (90 m) each (used doubled).

NEEDLES: Size 9 (5.5 mm): 16" (40-cm) circular (cir). Adjust needle size if necessary to obtain the correct gauge.

NOTIONS: Open-ring marker; tapestry needle; black sewing thread; beeswax to strengthen thread; sharp-point sewing needle; one ½" (1.3 cm) pearl drop (available at fabric or craft stores).

GAUGE: 12 sts and 16 rows = 4" (10 cm) with yarn doubled.

STITCH GUIDE
(See Glossary for illustrations of all of these techniques.)

Purl Lifted Increase: Insert right needle from top into purl st below needle, purl this st, then purl the st on needle.

Left Lifted Increase: Knit st on needle, with left needle, insert tip into back of the loop of st in row below st just knitted, knit this st.

Right Lifted Increase: Insert right needle into the back of the loop of the st in row below next st, knit this st, knit st on needle.

Vertical Double Decrease: Sl 2 sts tog knitwise, k1, psso.

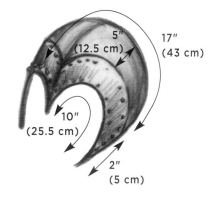

5" (12.5 cm)

17" (43 cm)

10" (25.5 cm)

2" (5 cm)

BORDER

With 2 strands of black held tog and using the long-tail method (see Glossary, page 131), CO 59 sts.

Row 1: (WS) P2tog, purl to last 2 sts, ssp (see Glossary, page 133)—57 sts rem.

Row 2: Ssk, k24, sl 3 sts tog kwise, k2tog, p3sso (pass the sts over one at a time to make this easier), k24, k2tog—51 sts rem.

Rows 3, 5, and 7: P2tog, [p4, purl lifted inc (see Stitch Guide) in next st] 4 times, p2, **sl 2 sts individually kwise, pass these 2 sts back to left needle, with yarn in front, insert right needle into these 2 sts from the back (as if to ssp), return the sts to the left needle (twisting them), p3tog (2 twisted sts plus next st)**, p2, [purl lifted inc in next st, p4] 4 times, ssp—55 sts.

Rows 4, 6, and 8: Ssk, k24, work vertical double dec (see Stitch Guide), k24, k2tog—51 sts rem.

Row 9: P2tog, p22, rep from ** to ** in Row 3, purl to last 2 sts, ssp—47 sts rem.

Row 10: Ssk, k20, work vertical double dec, k20, k2tog—43 sts rem.

Loosely BO all sts pwise.

SKULLCAP

With 2 strands of blue held tog and RS facing, pick up and knit 1 st in back loop of each BO sts of border—43 sts. Sl 1, purl to end. Place open-ring marker in center st (22nd st from each edge). Cont as foll, working short rows (see Glossary, page 136) as specified:

Row 1: (RS) Sl 1, right lifted inc in next st, k18, work vertical double dec, k18, left lifted inc in next st, k1—43 sts.

Rows 2 and 4: Sl 1, purl to end.

Row 3: Sl 1, k19 (1 st before marked center st), vertical double dec, knit to end—41 sts.

Row 5: Sl 1, right lifted inc, knit to 1 st before marked center st, vertical double dec, knit to last 2 sts, left lifted inc, k1.

Row 6: (short row) Sl 1, purl to last 3 sts, wrap next st, turn work, k16 (1 st before marked center st), vertical double dec, k16 to last 3 sts, wrap next st, turn work, purl to end, hiding wraps as you go—39 sts rem.

Row 7: Sl 1, knit to 1 st before marked center st, vertical double dec, knit to end, hiding wraps as you go—37 sts rem.

Row 8: (short row) Sl 1, purl to last 3 sts, wrap next st, turn work, k14 (1 st before marked center st), vertical double dec, k14 to last 3 sts, wrap next st, turn work, purl to end, hiding wraps as you go—35 sts rem.

Row 9: Sl 1, right lifted inc, knit to 1 st before marked center st, vertical double dec, knit to last 2 sts, hiding wraps as you go, left lifted inc, k1.

Row 10: (short row) Sl 1, purl to last 7 sts, wrap next st, turn work, k9 (1 st before marked center st), vertical double dec, knit to last 7 sts, wrap next st, turn work, purl to last 9 sts, wrap next st, turn work, k6 (1 st before marked center st), vertical double dec, knit 6 sts

to last 9 sts, wrap next st, turn work, purl to end, hiding wraps as you go—31 sts rem.

Row 11: Sl 1, knit to 1 st before marked center st, vertical double dec, knit to end, hiding wraps row as you go—29 sts rem.

Row 12: (short row) Sl 1, purl to last 9 sts, wrap next st, turn, k4 (1 st before marked center st), vertical double dec, knit to last 9 sts, wrap next st, turn, purl to end, hiding wraps as you go—27 sts rem.

Row 13: (short row) Sl 1, right lifted inc, k5, wrap next st, turn, purl to end.

Row 14: (short row) Sl 1, k5, wrap next st, turn, purl to end.

Row 15: Sl 1, right lifted inc, k11 (hiding wraps as you go) to 1 st before marked center st, vertical double dec, knit to last 2 sts, left lifted inc, k1—28 sts.

Row 16: (short row) Sl 1, p7, wrap next st, turn, knit to last 2 sts, left lifted inc, k1—29 sts.

Row 17: (short row) Sl 1, p6, wrap next st, turn, knit to end.

Row 18: Sl 1, purl to end, hiding wraps as you go.

FINISHING

Using the three-needle method (see Glossary, page 129), BO rem sts tog as foll: Sl 1, knit to center marked st, place previous 14 sts onto one dpn, place center st on open-ring marker to hold, rotate dpn counterclockwise so that WS of sts face tog (the seam will be on the RS of work, creating a ridge). Remove marker from center st, and place st on an empty dpn. Hold the dpn with center st in right hand, and the other 2 needles each holding 14 sts in the left hand, slip the first 2 sts (1 from each needle) together to right needle (3 sts on right needle), pass the center st over *both* slipped sts (2 sts on right needle); knit first st from each left needle together (3 sts on right needle), pass the 2 slipped sts over the new st to BO. Use the standard three-needle technique to BO rem sts tog. Cut yarn, draw tail through rem loop, and pull tight to secure. Weave in loose ends. With 2 strands of white threaded on a tapestry needle, make French knots (see Glossary, page 133) spaced about ½" (1.3 cm) apart around edge of black border. Cut a length of sewing thread and draw through a disk of beeswax to coat. "Press" the thread by *quickly* pulling it under a hot iron. With sewing needle and waxed thread, sew pearl drop onto center back point at nape of cap.

Renaissance Beret

The beret is a millinery fashion classic. First worn by the ancient Greeks some 2,500 years ago, the fashion migrated all over Europe, with early Greek and Roman traders taking the beret into the Basque country, which became its permanent home. With its round flat crown and usually made of wool, the Basque beret is well known. In adaptations, it has been slashed, jeweled, feathered, worn at angles with and without plumes, and made in all colors.

Completing one's costume with a beret was popularized in the Renaissance, especially by Rembrandt van Rijn. As an artist, I wonder, "If I dressed like him, could I also paint like him?" Probably not, but I can have an elegant beret knitted in rayon chenille, shaped full with the gathers draping softly, and worn to the side. A very real fashion statement or for make-believe . . . you decide!

Renaissance Beret

This hat is worked in the round from the brim (or band) to the top, then slightly felted to improve the drape. A ribbon band is sewn to the inside of the hatband to add stability.

FINISHED SIZE: About 22 to 23" (56 to 58.5 cm) circumference.

YARN: About 244 yd (223 m) of worsted-weight (Medium #4) yarn.
We used: Muench Touch Me (72% viscose/microfiber, 28% wool; 61 yd [55 m]/50 g): #3633 dark green, 244 yd (223 m).

NEEDLES: Size 6 (4 mm): 16" (40-cm) circular (cir) and set of 4 or 5 double-pointed (dpn). Size 8 (5 mm) for casting on. Adjust needle size if necessary to obtain the correct gauge.

NOTIONS: Markers (m); open-ring markers; tapestry needle; ¾ yd (68.5 cm) of 1" (2.5-cm) -wide velvet ribbon for hatband; sharp-point sewing needle; beeswax for strengthening sewing thread.

GAUGE: 15 sts and 20 rnds = 4" (10 cm) in St st worked in the rnd on size 6 (4 mm) needles (see Glossary, page 134, for working gauge swatches in the rnd).

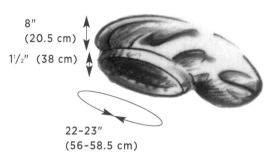

8" (20.5 cm)

1½" (38 cm)

22-23" (56-58.5 cm)

BAND

With larger needle, CO 86 sts. Change to smaller cir needle, place marker (pm), and join for working in the rnd, being careful not to twist sts.

Next rnd: *K1, p1; rep from * to end of rnd.

Work even in St st (knit every rnd) until piece measures 1½" (3.8 cm) from CO.

Inc rnd: *K1f&b (See Glossary, page 135); rep from * to end of rnd—172 sts. Knit even until piece measures 5" (12.5 cm) from inc rnd, or 6½" (16.5 cm) from CO, dec 2 sts evenly spaced on last rnd—170 sts rem.

CROWN

Work as foll:

Dec rnd 1: *K15, k2tog, pm; rep from * to end of rnd— 160 sts rem.

Place open-ring marker in work to indicate dec rnd.

Work even in St st until piece measures 1" (2.5 cm) from dec rnd, or 7½" (19 cm) from CO. Cont as foll:

Dec rnd 2: *K14, k2tog, slip marker (sl m); rep from *— 150 sts rem.

Place second open-ring marker to indicate dec rnd.
Knit 2 rnds even.

Dec rnd 3: *K13, k2tog; rep from * to end of rnd—140 sts rem.

Place third open-ring marker to indicate dec rnd. Knit 2 rnds even. Cont to dec every rnd as foll, changing to dpn when necessary.

Dec rnd 4: *K5, k2tog; rep from * to end of rnd—120 sts rem.

Dec rnd 5: *K4, k2tog; rep from * to end of rnd—100 sts rem.

Dec rnd 6: *K3, k2tog; rep from * to end of rnd—80 sts rem.

Dec rnd 7: *K2, k2tog; rep from * to end of rnd—60 sts rem.

Dec rnd 8: *K1, k2tog; rep from * to end of rnd—40 sts rem.

Dec rnd 9: *K2tog; rep from * to end of rnd—20 sts rem. Remove all markers. Cut yarn, thread tail on tapestry needle, draw tail through rem loops, and pull tight to secure.

FINISHING

Weave in loose ends.

Felting: Felt according to the instructions on page 134, to keep rayon chenille stable and prevent worming. (*Note:* shrinkage is only about 5 percent and will not affect the size.)

Ribbon band: Cut velvet ribbon to head circumference plus 2" (5 cm). Allowing for a 1" (2.5-cm) seam allowance at each end of ribbon, sew ribbon into a ring that matches head circumference. Pin WS of ribbon ring to WS of hat, aligning lower edge of ribbon with lower edge of hat. Cut a length of sewing thread and draw through a disk of beeswax to coat. "Press" the thread by *quickly* pulling it under a hot iron. With waxed sewing thread and sharp-point needle, use a whipstitch (see Glossary, page 139) to sew both edges of ribbon ring to inside brim.

Hunter's Fedora

The fedora is said to have been named after *Fedora*, a popular nineteenth-century play by the French playwright Victorien Sardou. A felt fedora tops off the traditional dress—short leather trousers, knee stockings, heavy hobnail shoes, decorated shirts, embroidered suspenders, and jacket—of Bavarian mountaineers.

The wool and flax yarn I have chosen felts beautifully in this hat to a heathered finish. I tend to like this hat without a hatband, but you can opt for some leather with a feather! Look out, Indiana Jones!

Hunter's Fedora

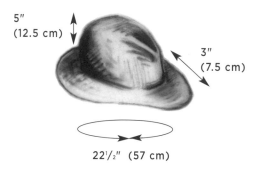

5"
(12.5 cm)

3"
(7.5 cm)

22¹/₂" (57 cm)

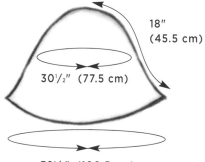

18"
(45.5 cm)

30¹/₂" (77.5 cm)

39¹/₂" (100.5 cm)

This hat is worked in the round from the brim to the top, then felted and shaped.

FINISHED SIZE: About 22½" (57 cm) circumference and 5" (12.5 cm) tall; brim is about 3" (7.5 cm) wide.

YARN: About 490 yd (448 m) of worsted-weight (Medium #4) yarn.
We used: Harrisville Flax & Wool (20% flax, 80% wool; 245 yd [224 m]/100 g): #221 moss, 490 yd (448 m).

NEEDLES: Size 10½ (6.5 mm): 24" (60-cm) circular (cir) and set of 4 or 5 double-pointed (dpn). Adjust needle size if necessary to obtain the correct gauge.

NOTIONS: Markers (m); 2 coilless safety pins; tapestry needle.

GAUGE: 20 sts and 24 rnds = 6" (15 cm) in St st worked in the rnd, before felting (see Glossary, page 134, for working gauge swatches in the rnd).

BRIM

With cir needle, CO 132 sts. Place marker (pm) to de-
note center back and join for working in the rnd, being
careful not to twist sts. *Next rnd:* K33, pm, k66, pm,
k33. Slip markers every rnd. Knit 3 rnds even. Dec as
foll:
Dec rnd 1: K36, [k2tog, k4] 10 times, k36—122 sts rem.
Knit 7 rnds even.
Dec rnd 2: [K2tog, k4] 5 times, k6 to m, [k2tog, k3] 10
   times, k6, [k2tog, k4] 5 times—102 sts rem.
Knit 7 rnds even.
Dec rnd 3: [K2tog, k8] 10 times, k2tog—92 sts rem.
   Place a coilless pin to mark this rnd.
Knit even until piece measures 9½" (24 cm) from coil-
less pin. Remove coilless pin.

CROWN

Dec for crown as foll, changing to dpn when necessary:
Rnd 1: [K7, k2tog] 10 times, k2tog—81 sts rem.
Rnds 2, 4, 6, 8, 10, and 12: Knit.
Rnd 3: [K6, k2tog] 10 times, k1—71 sts rem.
Rnd 5: [K5, k2tog] 10 times, k1—61 sts rem.
Rnd 7: [K4, k2tog] 10 times, k1—51 sts rem.
Rnd 9: [K3, k2tog] 10 times, k1—41 sts rem.
Rnd 11: [K2, k2tog] 10 times, k1—31 sts rem.
Rnd 13: [K1, k2tog] 9 times, [k2tog] 2 times—20 sts
   rem.

FINISHING

Place 10 sts each on 2 dpn. With yarn threaded on a
tapestry needle and using the Kitchener st (see
Glossary, page 139), graft sts tog. Weave in loose ends.

Place coilless safety pin at center back to enable you to
shape the felted piece accurately.
Felting: Felt according to the instructions on page 134 (I
felted this one by machine) until hat folded flat measures
11" (28 cm) to 11½" (29 cm) at base of crown. Rinse out
soap and blot out excess water with bath towels.
Shaping: Holding top of crown, pull brim downward to
smooth lengthwise grain of knitting around entire brim.
Fold hat at marked center back and make a crease to define the center front of hat. Place a coilless pin at base of
crown at center front. Shape round dome of crown on
your head, a hat form, or a bowl that is the perfect size.
When roundness is achieved, lay hat on flat surface and
shape brim by rolling up hatback and sides slightly,
without stretching the edge of the brim, and taper roll
to nothing at the center front. With the side of your
flattened palm, make an indentation on the top of the
crown along the back/front axis. If necessary, lift up the
hat and restore the crown curve at the back of the indentation. Pinch hat sides on both sides of center front
to create a sharper tripartite definition at the front of
the crown.

King Edward VI Brimmed Beret

I n the sixteenth century, King Edward VI popularized a beret with a brim very similar to the brim of a British beefeater (a flat-topped crown of medium height gathered into a headband with a medium-wide brim)—a black beaver hat that originated in the same period and was worn then by British yeomen and warders of the Tower of London.

   The llama/wool blend I have used produces supple gathers and luxurious warmth. I've contemporized the overall shape, softening the crown and securing the outer edge of the brim with an upturned edge, but I have remained true to the hat's original character. King Edward VI may not be remembered as a fashion icon, but the silhouette of his beret truly transcends the ages.

King Edward VI Brimmed Beret

This hat is worked in the round, beginning with the crown. Then stitches for the brim are picked up along the edge of the crown, and the brim is worked downward to the lower edge.

FINISHED SIZE: Crown circumference: to fit 22 to 23" (56 to 58.5 cm) head.

YARN: About 254 yd (232 m) of chunky (Bulky #5) yarn. *We used:* Classic Elite Montera (50% llama, 50%wool, 127 yd [116 m]/100 g): #3813 black, 254 yd (232 m).

NEEDLES: Size 9 (5.5 mm): 16" (40-cm) circular (cir) and set of 5 double-pointed (dpn). Adjust needle size if necessary to obtain the correct gauge.

NOTIONS: Marker (m); tapestry needle; 34" (86.5 cm) plastic boning to shape brim (available at fabric and craft stores); about 8" (20.5 cm) smooth cotton yarn for knitted cord provisional CO; size J/9 (5.5 mm) crochet hook.

GAUGE: 16 sts and 20 rnds = 4" (10 cm) in St st worked in the rnd (see Glossary, page 134, for working gauge swatches in the rnd).

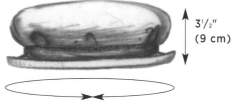

3¹/₂" (9 cm)

22-23" (56-58.5 cm)

CROWN

With cir needle, CO 80 sts. Place marker and join for working in the rnd, being careful not to twist sts. Knit 2 rnds even. Inc as foll:

Inc rnd 1: *K3, work lifted inc (see Glossary, page 136) in next st; rep from * to end of rnd—100 sts.

Knit 2 rnds even.

Inc rnd 2: *K4, lifted inc in next st; rep from * to end of rnd—120 sts.

Knit even until piece measures 3½" (9 cm) from CO. Dec as foll:

Dec rnd 1: [K10, k2tog] 10 times—110 sts rem.

Knit 1 rnd even.

Dec rnd 2: [K9, k2tog] 10 times—100 sts rem.

Knit 1 rnd even.

Cont in this manner, knitting 1 st fewer between decs every other rnd until 20 sts rem. *Next rnd:* *K2tog; rep from * to end of rnd—10 sts rem.

Cut yarn, thread tail on tapestry needle, draw through rem sts, and pull tight to secure. Weave in loose ends.

BRIM

With cir needle and RS facing, pick up and knit 80 sts in unused loops of CO edge. Knit 2 rnds even. Inc as foll:

Inc rnd 1: *K3, lifted inc in next st; rep from * to end of rnd—100 sts.

Knit 2 rnds even.

Inc rnd 2: *K4, lifted inc in next st; rep from * to end of rnd—120 sts.

Knit even until piece measures 3¾" (9.5 cm) from pick-up rnd. BO all sts.

FINISHING

Boning: Shape plastic boning into a ring, overlapping ½" (1.3 cm). Machine zigzag or hand sew in place. Place boning on knit side along outer edge of brim and fold brim edge up and over boning toward hat center (purl sts will be visible on RS of work). With yarn threaded on a tapestry needle, use a whipstitch (see Glossary, page 139) to sew boning in place.

Knitted cord band: With dpn and using a crochet chain provisional method (see Glossary, page 130), CO 4 sts. Work 4-st knitted cord (see Glossary, page 137) until piece measures about 22" (56 cm), or length to fit comfortably around head. Remove provisional CO and use Kitchener st (see Glossary, page 139) to graft cord ends into a ring. Place knitted-cord band around hat at boundary between crown and brim, and with yarn threaded on a tapestry needle and working with WS of hat facing you, use a backstitch (see Glossary, page 138) to stitch in place.

Glengarry

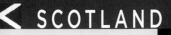

The glengarry is the old bluebonnet of the Highlanders—so-called because it has always been made of blue wool—but folded to make a crease in the top. A little blue or red tuft in the glengarry signified a clan chief. Traditionally, the glengarry has stiff sides and is banded with a plaid tartan pattern of the Stuart colors to memorialize Bonnie Prince Charlie.

With a bit of short-row engineering, I shaped this hat and knitted it all in one piece, with a center top graft to finish it off. The merino-and-silk yarn I used presents a fine dark blue heather for the traditional main color, complemented by red and white.

Glengarry

This hat is worked in the round from the sideband to the center top, and is shaped with short rows.

FINISHED SIZE: About 22½" (57 cm) circumference and 4" (10 cm) tall at highest point of side.

YARN: About 218 yd (199 m) of main color and 109 yd (100 m) each of two contrasting colors of DK-weight (Light #3) yarn. *We used:* Naturally Merino et Soie (70% New Zealand wool, 30% silk; 109 yd [100 m]/100 g): #108 very dark blue, 218 yd (199 m); #103 white and #107 red, 109 yd (100 m) each.

NEEDLES: Size 6 (4 mm): 16" (40-cm) circular (cir). Adjust needle size if necessary to obtain the correct gauge. Spare set of straight needles for Kitchener finishing.

NOTIONS: Markers (m); tapestry needle.

GAUGE: 20 sts and 28 rnds = 4" (10 cm) in St st worked in the rnd (see Glossary, page 134 for working gauge swatches in the rnd).

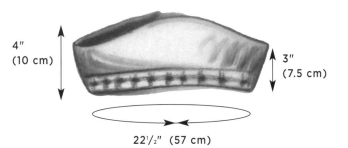

4" (10 cm)

3" (7.5 cm)

22½" (57 cm)

SIDEBAND

With dark blue, CO 112 sts. Place marker (pm) to denote cap back and join for working in the rnd, being careful not to twist sts. Purl 1 rnd. Work color work band as foll:

Rnd 1: *K3 white, sl 1 dark blue; rep from * to end of rnd.

Rnd 2: *K3 white, k1 red; rep from * to end of rnd.

Rnd 3: *K3 dark blue, p1 red; rep from * to end of rnd.

Rnd 4: *K3 white, k1 dark blue; rep from * to end of rnd.

Rnd 5: *K3 white, sl 1 dark blue; rep from * to end of rnd.

Cut off white and red. Cont with dark blue as foll: Knit 1 rnd, purl 1 rnd. *Next rnd:* K57, pm, k55, remove m from beg of rnd, k1, pm (the beg of rnd is moved forward by 1 st). Make ridges at center front and center back as foll:

Rnd 1: K53, pm, vertical double dec (sl 2 sts tog kwise, k1, p2sso; see Glossary, page 133), k53, vertical double dec—108 sts rem.

Rnd 2: *K53, lift a stitch from behind the front st of the double dec and knit it, knit the center st of the double dec, lift up the other st from behind the center st and knit it; rep from *—112 sts.

Rep these 2 rnds 4 more times, ending with Rnd 2—112 sts; piece should measure about 3" (7.5 cm) from CO. Remove marker, slip last st of rnd from right needle onto left needle, replace m onto right needle (marker now immediately follows the raised center st of vertical double dec), transfer slipped st back to right needle and count as first st of the 48 sts to be knit as short rows. Work short rows (see Glossary, page 136) as foll:

Short-row 1: K48, wrap next st, turn.

Short-row 2: P41, wrap next st, turn.

Short-row 3: K34, wrap next st, turn.

Short-row 4: P27, wrap next st, turn.

Short-row 5: K20, wrap next st, turn.

Short-row 6: P13, wrap next st, turn.

Short-row 7: K35, working wraps tog with wrapped sts as you go, ending at center front—one side completed. (*Note:* This will hide only half of the wraps; the remaining wraps are picked up after the short-row shaping on the other side of hat.)

Move center front marker 1 st to the right where it now immediately follows the raised center st of the vertical double dec. The st in front of the marker is now the first st in the rnd. Beg at center front, rep Short-rows 1–7 once to work the second side of hat, ending at center back. Knit 1 rnd, working rem wraps tog with wrapped sts as you go, keeping marker in place.

CROWN

Purl 1 row for turning ridge. Beg at center back marker, k38, wrap next st, turn, p22, wrap next st, turn, k24, wrap next st, turn, p26, wrap next st, turn, k28, wrap next st, turn. Cont in this manner, working 2 more sts each row until you work the last 2 rows of this side as foll: P54, remove m and wrap center st, replace m, turn work, k56 (all sts on one side of crown). Hide wraps as you go by working them tog with wrapped sts. Rep from * for second side until you work k56 sts.

FINISHING

With WS tog, place 56 sts of each half of crown onto a straight needle for finishing, hold needles parallel making sure needle points are toward the working yarn. With yarn threaded on a tapestry needle and using the Kitchener st (see Glossary, page 139), graft sts tog. Weave in loose ends. If necessary, steam WS of tartan border manipulating work to prevent a wavy edge. Turn hat to RS. Fold center top down along turning ridges and steam lightly (sides should lay flat).

Cable Braid

The Emerald Isle has produced a wealth of beautiful cabled knit stitches for the world to admire, reproduce, and proudly wear. While they obviously reflect the ropes that are so much a part of the lives of a fishing community, cable designs have been part of Irish artistic culture since the first torques (neck rings made of gold or bronze wire twisted into a rope) were made by the Celts in the sixth century B.C.

Using the cable idea, I have braided a cable from knitted strips and hand-stitched the braid onto a ribbed stocking-hat foundation. The off-white wool made famous by knitters on the Aran Isles gives the hat a distinctive Irish flavor.

Cable Braid

This hat is worked in the round from the brim/sides to the center top. The cable braid is worked in three separate strips that are braided together, then sewn to the crown.

FINISHED SIZE: About 20" (51 cm) circumference (stretches to 23" [58.5 cm]) and 7" (18 cm) tall. Each strip for cable braid measures 3" (7.5 cm) wide, before braiding.

YARN: About 360 yd (329 m) of worsted-weight (Medium #4) yarn.
We used: Jamieson Soft Shetland (100% Shetland wool; 120 yd [109 m]/2 oz): #104 natural white, 360 yd (329 m).

NEEDLES: Crown and Cable Braid Strips—Size 8 (5 mm): set of 4 or 5 double-pointed (dpn). Crown Shaping—Size 6 (4 mm): set of 4 or 5 dpn. Adjust needle size if necessary to obtain the correct gauge.

NOTIONS: Marker (m); tapestry needle; long straight pins with colored heads.

GAUGE: Lower Crown: 20 sts and 22 rnds = 4" (10 cm) in k2, p2 rib worked in the rnd on larger needles, stretched (see Glossary, page 134, for working gauge swatches in the rnd).

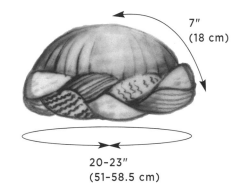

7"
(18 cm)

20–23"
(51–58.5 cm)

CROWN

With larger needles, CO 112 sts. Place marker (pm) and join for working in the rnd, being careful not to twist sts. Work k2, p2 rib until piece measures 6" (15 cm) from CO. Change to smaller needles. *Dec rnd:* *K2tog, p2tog; rep from *—56 sts rem. Work k1, p1 rib until piece measures 1" (2.5 cm) from dec rnd. *Next rnd:* *Ssk (see Glossary, page 132); rep from *—28 sts rem. Cut yarn, thread tail on a tapestry needle, draw through rem sts, and pull tight to secure.

CABLE BRAID

Work 3 strips back and forth as foll:

Strip 1: With larger needles, CO 12 sts. Work garter st (knit every row) until piece measures 25" (63.5 cm) from beg. BO all sts.

Strip 2: With larger needles, CO 12 sts. Work seed st as foll:

Row 1: *K1, p1; rep from * to end of row.

Row 2: P1, k1; rep from * to end of row.

Rep Rows 1 and 2 until piece measures 25" (63.5 cm) from beg. BO all sts.

Strip 3: With larger needles, CO 18 sts. Work k2, p2 rib until piece measures 25" (63.5 cm) from beg. BO all sts.

FINISHING

Stack the three strips, one on top of another and pin tog along short ends of all 3 strips (Figure 1). Loosely braid the strips, keeping each strip as flat as possible. With yarn threaded on a tapestry needle, sew the BO edge of each strip to its CO edge to form a ring. Adjust braid to hide seams. Place crown over a hat form or bowl of appropriate size, and pin braid for placement to lower edge of crown so lower edge of ribbed crown is hidden under the braid. Turn crown inside out, place over the hat form or bowl again, and with yarn threaded on a tapestry needle, work 2 rows of herringbone st to sew braid onto crown along center and near top of braid (Figure 2).

FINISHING

Figure 2

Figure 1

Soft Winter Snowflakes

Sisu is the Finnish word for courage and strength. Almost one-third of the Finnish land mass is north of the Arctic Circle, and it takes a people of strong character to thrive in winters whose average temperature is −8°F (−22°C). The aurora borealis— flashes of light in the night sky—is a dramatic feature of Finnish winters, and for my hat I've combined the look of lights in a dusky sky with the traditional snowflakes of Scandinavian knitting design. I've shaped the snowflake band to fit the contours of the head and frame the face, and I've softly gathered the full crown into a braided tassel. Winter Snowflakes is an elegant take on Scandinavian tradition.

Soft Winter Snowflakes

This hat begins with the facing for the Fair Isle band (worked back and forth in rows), followed by the patterned band. Stitches are then added for the back of the hat and the loose-fitting crown is worked in the round and shaped with decreases. A braid decorates the hat back. The hat is worn with front band draped around the face (which holds the hat in place) and the crown at the back of the head.

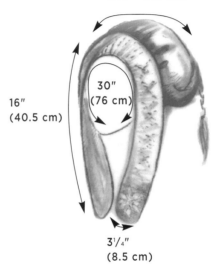

FINISHED SIZE: About 30" (76 cm) circumference and 11½" (29 cm) wide, measured from center front to center back, including front band.

YARN: About 440 yd (402 m) of main color and 220 yd (201 m) of contrast color of worsted-weight (Medium #4) yarn. *We used:* Cascade Cascade 220 (100% wool, 220 yd [201 m]/100 g): #9327 blue, 440 yd (402 m); #8010 off-white, 220 yd (201 m).

NEEDLES: Size 7 (4.5 mm): 24" (60-cm) circular (cir) and set of 4 or 5 double-pointed (dpn). Size 6 (4 mm): 24" (60-cm) cir. Size 2 or 3 (2.75 or 3.25 mm): 24" (60-cm) or longer cir. Adjust needle size if necessary to obtain the correct gauge.

NOTIONS: Markers (m); tapestry needle.

GAUGE: 20 sts and 24 rows = 4" (10 cm) in St st on larger needles.

Snowflake

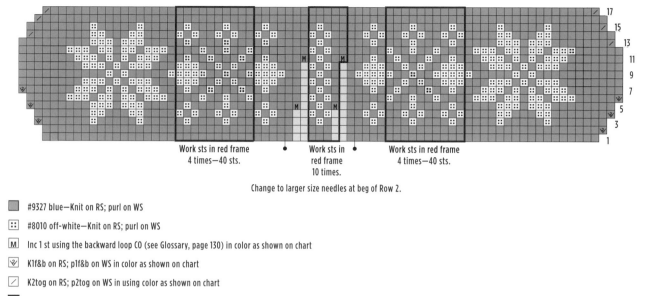

Work sts in red frame
4 times—40 sts.

Work sts in
red frame
10 times.

Work sts in red frame
4 times—40 sts.

Change to larger size needles at beg of Row 2.

▨ #9327 blue—Knit on RS; purl on WS

▦ #8010 off-white—Knit on RS; purl on WS

M Inc 1 st using the backward loop CO (see Glossary, page 130) in color as shown on chart

◈ K1f&b on RS; p1f&b on WS in color as shown on chart

╱ K2tog on RS; p2tog on WS in using color as shown on chart

■ Pattern repeat

☐ No stitch

• Marker

SHAPED FACING AND SNOWFLAKE BAND

With blue, larger cir needle, and using the long-tail method (see Glossary, page 131), *loosely* CO 174 sts. Work back and forth in rows as foll:

Row 1: (WS) Purl to last st, p1f&b—175 sts.

Row 2: (RS) Knit to last st, k1f&b—176 sts.

Repeat these 2 rows 2 more times—180 sts. *Next row:* (WS) P62, place marker (pm), p56, pm, p62. *Next row:* (RS) K62, sl marker (sl m), k2, [k3, k2tog] 10 times, k4, sl m, k62—170 sts rem. Work even in St st until piece measures 2" (5 cm) from CO, ending with a WS row. *Next row:* (RS) K2tog, k60, sl m, k2, [k2, k2tog] 10 times, k4, sl m, k62—159 sts rem. *Next row:* (WS)

P2tog, purl to end of row—158 sts rem. Cont in St st, dec 1 st at beg of next 4 rows in this manner, ending with a WS row completed. Remove markers—154 sts rem; piece should measure about 3" (7.5 cm) from CO.

Turning ridge: Change to smaller cir needle, knit 1 row.

Next row: (WS) Knit 1 row on WS to create turning ridge.

Color work band: With RS facing, work Row 1 of Snowflake chart, placing 2 markers as shown on chart (for later BO reference). Change to larger needles. Work Rows 2–17 of chart, joining white on Row 3, and working increases, decreases, and color patt as indicated—176 sts after Row 17. Leave working yarn attached.

Join facing to band: With smallest cir needle, pick up (but do not knit) 174 loops from CO edge of facing. (*Note:* When working the following instructions, it is easier to knit the CO loops through the back loop when joining the loops tog with the sts from the snowflake side.) With WS side of snowflake toward you, fold facing along turning ridge so that WS face tog. With needle holding the 174 CO loops in front, and needle holding the 176 snowflake sts in back (the working yarn will be on the back needle), use the three-needle method (see Glossary, page 129) to BO the CO loops tog with the live sts as foll: BO 50 sts, then without BO more sts, k1 st from each needle tog to m (11 sts on right needle), sl m, knit 1 loop from front needle tog with 2 sts from snowflake needle (1 st dec from snowflake side), *knit 1 st from each needle tog; rep from * to 2 sts before next m on snowflake needle, knit 1 loop from front needle tog with 2 sts from snowflake needle (1 st dec from snowflake side; 52 sts between m on snowflake side), sl m, k1 st from each needle tog until there are 11 sts from m.

Prepare for BO: Knit 1 st from each needle tog 2 more times, and using the first of these 2 sts, BO rem sts to end of row—74 sts rem on needle. Cut yarn and draw tail through rem st to secure.

GATHERED HAT BACK

Note: Use the backward loop CO (see Glossary, page 130) for all increases (inc 1). Lay snowflake band out flat, with snowflakes facing up to refer to left and right side of needle. With blue, larger needle, and using the long-tail method, CO 30 sts onto left needle tip as shown above. Turn work and purl these 30 sts. *Next row:* (RS) [K3, inc 1] 9 times across 27 of the 30 new sts, k3; cont across next 74 sts as foll: [k2, inc 1] 37 times—

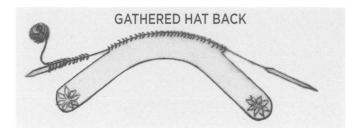

GATHERED HAT BACK

150 sts total. Pm, and join for working in the rnd. Work even in rnds for 8" (20.5 cm).

Decrease for back:

Rnd 1: *K1, k2tog; rep from * to end of rnd—100 sts rem.

Rnds 2 and 5: *K1 blue, k1 white; rep from * to end of rnd.

Rnds 3 and 6: Knit all sts with blue.

Rnd 4: With blue, *k2tog; rep from * to end of rnd—50 sts rem.

Rnd 7: Rep Rnd 4—25 sts rem.

Rnd 8: *K1 blue, k1 white; rep from * to last st, end k1 blue (the first and last sts are blue). Cut off white.

Rnd 9: With blue, *k2tog; rep from * to last st, k1—13 sts rem.

Cut yarn, thread tail on a tapestry needle, draw through rem sts, and pull tight to secure.

FINISHING

Embroidery: With blue threaded on a tapestry needle, work blanket st edging around the short curved sides of the snowflake "strap" as described in box on page 81.

Braided tassel: Cut 4 strands of blue and 2 strands of white, each 36" (91.5 cm) long. Working at center back where all loops have been drawn up to close back of hat, thread all strands on tapestry needle and insert needle and threads through to WS just right of exact center, and back through to RS just left of exact center as shown at right. Divide the strands into one section of 4 white strands and two sections of 4 blue strands each, and work the three groups into a braid for 6" (15 cm). Tie an overhand knot at end of braid to secure the ends. Trim ends to 3" (7.5 cm).

Lightly steam snowflake band and gathered back. Gently pull on braid to encourage gathers to radiate from the snowflake band into the hat fabric. Let dry to set.

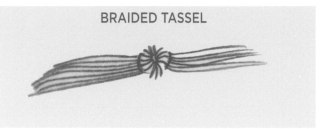
BRAIDED TASSEL

BLANKET STITCH EDGING

With RS facing and leaving a tail to work in later, insert needle from back to front at left corner of curve. Work 1 whipstitch in the same corner to anchor the yarn. Insert needle just to right of whipstitch from front to back making sure needle passes in front of yarn to create edge (Figure 1). Cont in this manner, working from left to right along curved edge (Figure 2). Secure last st by inserting needle into work just behind last st (Figures 3 and 4). Hide yarn tails under WS of blanket st.

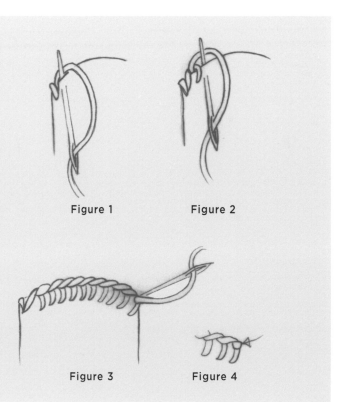

Figure 1   Figure 2

Figure 3   Figure 4

Four Winds Hat

L apland lies in the extreme northern part of Finland. It's a remote country that stretches from northern Norway to northern Russia. Lapp costume is one of the most ancient of western Europe that resisted cultural change because of the country's isolation. Both weather and way of life make the Lapp folk costume strictly practical.

The Four-Cornered Hat represents the four corners of the earth, which the ancient Lapps thought was square. Traditionally the hat was made in blue wool to symbolize the sky, and the headband was often made of reindeer fur or embellished colorfully with red, yellow, and white wool. The four points were stuffed with down to maintain their shape and keep out the cold.

Four Winds Hat

Knitting this hat is an adventure using some familiar shaping and construction techniques in an innovative way. I have devised a way to shape and connect all four points with only two ends to weave in when the knitting is complete. The band embroidery is extra. Blue is traditional, but you'll be the envy of other fans if you use the colors of your favorite athletic team.

This hat is worked in the round in one piece from the lower edge to the base of the points, then the points are worked separately to the tip, and shaped with short rows.

FINISHED SIZE: About 22" (56 cm) circumference and 7½" (19 cm) tall.

YARN: About 132 yd (120 m) of chunky (Bulky #5) yarn and a few yards (meters) of two contrasting colors of worsted-weight (Medium #4) yarn.
We used: Brown Sheep Burly Spun (100% wool; 132 yd [120 m]/8 oz): #BS-79 blue boy, 132 yd (120 m).
Brown Sheep Lamb's Pride Superwash Worsted (100% wool; 200 yd [183 m]/100 g): #SW11 white and #SW14 yellow, a few yards (meters) each.

NEEDLES: Size 11 (8 mm): 24" (60-cm) and 16" (40-cm) circular (cir) and set of 4 or 5 double-pointed (dpn). Adjust needle size if necessary to obtain the correct gauge.

NOTIONS: Markers (m); tapestry needle; small amounts of polyester stuffing to fill hat points.

GAUGE: 9 sts and 14 rnds = 4" (10 cm) in St st, worked in the rnd (see Glossary, page 134, for working gauge swatches in the rnd).

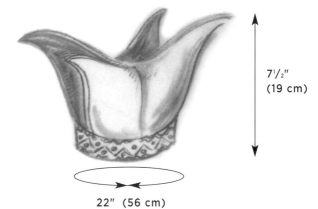

7½"
(19 cm)

22" (56 cm)

SIDEBAND

With shorter cir needle, CO 52 sts. Place marker (pm) and join for working in the rnd, being careful not to twist sts. Purl 1 rnd. Knit 1 rnd, ending 1 st before m (to avoid purl jog), sl 1 kwise, insert right needle tip into back loop of st below st on left needle, lift this loop and knit it and the slipped st on right needle together through back loops (as for ssk), temporarily removing marker to do so. Knit 2 rnds. Purl 1 rnd. Mark 4 sections as foll:

Rnd 1: [K6, sl 1 pwise, k6, pm] 4 times, working last st as before to avoid purl jog.

Rnd 2: Knit.

Rnd 3: [K6, sl 1 pwise, k6] 4 times.

Rnd 4: [Knit to 1 st before slipped st, work left lifted inc (see Glossary, page 136), sl 1, right lifted inc (see Glossary, page 136), knit to marker] 4 times—60 sts; 15 sts in each marked section.

Rnd 5: Knit.

Rep the last 2 rnds until there are 100 sts—25 sts in each marked section. *Next rnd:* [Ssk, knit, working lifted inc 1 st before and 1 st after center slipped st, knit to 2 sts before marker, k2tog] 4 times—still 100 sts. Change to longer cir needle. Knit 1 rnd even.

POINTS

Cont working 2 lifted incs on RS rows as established, work short rows (see Glossary, page 136) as foll:

Short-row 1: (RS) Knit to 3 sts before first marker, wrap next st, turn.

Short-row 2: (WS) Purl to 3 sts before marker, wrap next st, turn.

Short-row 3: Knit to 5 sts before marker, wrap next st, turn.

Short-row 4: Purl to 5 sts before marker, wrap next st, turn.

Short-row 5: Knit to 7 sts before marker, wrap next st, turn.

Short-row 6: Purl to 7 sts before marker, wrap next st, turn.

Next row: Knit to marker, working 2 lifted inc, and working wraps tog with wrapped sts as you go—end of first section; 33 sts in first section. Some wraps are still in place and will be hidden later.

Rep from Short-row 1 for the other 3 sections—132 sts total; 33 sts in each section.

FINISHING

Connect points: *Knit to center st of first section, working wraps tog with wrapped sts as you go, place 16 sts just worked onto a dpn, rotate dpn counterclockwise behind cir needle so WS of sts face each other, slip center st to empty dpn and use this needle and the three-needle method (see Glossary, page 129) to BO all sts to next marker (1 st rem on right needle from BO), k1 in next section (2 sts on right needle), BO last st of previous section—1 point complete. The next section beg with 1 st rem on right needle from BO; this st counts as the first of the 16 sts knit to the center st. Rep from * for each of the other 3 sections, knitting first st in each section to BO last st of previous point—1 st rem. Cut yarn, draw tail through rem loop, and pull tight to secure. With yarn threaded on a tapestry needle, close top opening by sewing top "seam" of each point tog at center. Weave in loose ends.

Embroidery: With white threaded on a tapestry needle, work long running sts to create zigzag along lower edge as foll: *insert threaded needle from WS near lower purl ridge, insert needle to WS near upper purl ridge 2 sts to the left, skip 2 sts; rep from *. Reverse direction and work long sts that slant in the opposite direction, matching point insertions. With yellow, make French knots (see Glossary, page 133) centered over center st in each triangle section created by zigzags. Weave in loose ends.

Zigs and Zags Stocking Hat

Bright yellow, red, and blue are the featured colors in hats from Lapland, with a pom-pom as a standard part of the regalia. The zigzag markings can be traced back to ancient Siberia, where primitive tailors cut similar designs from tanned skins and colored them.

I opted to apply the color banding as a separate piece in the overall design. Because they're sculptural and not knitted in, the small squares turned on point pick up on the ancient theme of the zigzag and add movement. I present this hat with large pom-pom in the traditional Lapp colors of yellow, red, and blue, as well as a more contemporary color palette that reminds me of a still winter evening.

Zigs and Zags Stocking Hat

This hat is worked in the round from the lower crown to the top. The diamond-shaped strips are knitted separately, then sewn to the hat.

FINISHED SIZE: About 22" (56 cm) circumference and 8" (20.5 cm) tall.

YARN: About 174 yd (159 m) of one main color and 87 yd (80 m) each of two contrasting colors of worsted-weight (Medium #4) yarn.
We used: Dale of Norway Free Style (100% wool, 87 yd [80 m]/50 g). **Version 1:** #0090 black (MC), 174 yd (159 m); #5533 blue (A) and #0010 white (B), 87 yd (80 m) each. **Version 2:** #5444 blue (MC), 174 yd (159 m); #4018 red (A) and #2427 yellow (B), 87 yd (80 m) each.

NEEDLES: Hat—Size 7 (4.5 mm): 16" (40 cm) circular (cir) and set of 4 or 5 double-pointed (dpn). Garter-stitch diamond strip—Size 6 (4 mm): straight. Adjust needle size if necessary to obtain the correct gauge.

NOTIONS: Tapestry needle; long sewing pins with colored heads; 4½" (11.5-cm) piece of cardboard to make pom-pom.

GAUGE: 18 sts and 24 rnds = 4" (10 cm) in St st worked in the rnd on larger needles (see Glossary, page 134, for working gauge swatches in the rnd).

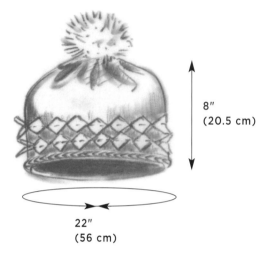

8"
(20.5 cm)

22"
(56 cm)

HAT SIDES

Braided trim: (worked on WS of hat) With A and B held tog and leaving 6" (15 cm) tail, make a slipknot and place on cir needle. Slipknot does not count as a st. With the working end of A over your thumb and B over your index finger, use the long-tail method (see Glossary, page 131) to CO 100 sts (B will form sts on the needle; A will form the ridge beneath the needle). Remove slipknot, slip the first st onto the right needle tip, bring both working yarns A and B to the front, return this st to left needle tip, turn work, hold yarn in back. Place marker (pm) and join, being careful not to twist sts. With WS facing, cont as foll:

Rnd 1: K1 A, *pick up B from *under* A and k1 B, pick up A from *under* B and k1 A; rep from * to end of rnd, twisting yarn at every color change.

Rnd 2: *Pick up A from *over* B and k1 A, pick up B from *over* A and k1 B; rep from * to end of rnd, picking up colors from *over* one another each time, thus untwisting yarns as you go.

Slip first st of rnd onto right needle, bring both working yarns A and B to the front of work, return this st to left needle, turn work to RS. Cut off A and B.

Sides: Join MC and knit every rnd until piece measures 7½" (19 cm) from beg.

CROWN

Dec for top as foll: *Next rnd:* *K2tog; rep from *—50 sts rem. *Next rnd:* *K2tog; rep from *—25 sts rem. Cut yarn, thread tail on a tapestry needle, draw through rem sts, and pull tight to secure.

GARTER STITCH DIAMONDS STRIP

With B and smaller needle, CO 6 sts. Knit 8 rows. Next row: *BO 5 sts—1 st rem. Turn work and use the backward loop method (see Glossary, page 130) to CO 5 more sts—6 sts total. Knit 7 rows. Rep from * until 16 diamonds have been made, ending by binding off all sts. Cut yarn, draw tail through last st, and pull tight to secure. Make another strip the same with A.

FINISHING

Pin diamond strip B to hat just above braided edge. With B threaded on a tapestry needle, use a backstitch (see Glossary, page 138) to sew in place as foll: Working through center of diamonds from side point to side point, make line of backstitches parallel to braided edge; top and bottom points of diamonds remain free and unstitched. Pin diamond strip A to hat just above strip B so that points match, and sew in place as for strip B.

Pom-pom: Holding A and B tog, wrap yarn around 4½" (11.5 cm) piece of cardboard 100 times. Cut 2 strands of A, each 18" (45.5 cm) long, and lay on flat surface. Slide pom-pom wraps off cardboard and lay perpendicularly over the 2 strands of A. Tie A strands tightly in a square knot around pom-pom wraps. Shake out pom-pom and trim to even, round shape. Fasten pom-pom to crown of hat with the 2 strands of A, and tie the 2 strands tog in a square knot on the WS of hat. Weave in loose ends.

Cossack

The Cossack hat is peerless among head coverings in the frigid north. For protection against Russia's piercing wind and cold, these tall fur hats range in size from thin fur coverings to thick, dense fur a foot tall. The wild horsemen of the steppes, later known as Cossacks, wore this hat and gave it its name. Under the czars, the Cossacks were organized into military units for border patrol work and their winter fur hats were eventually standardized. Today's Russian fur hat is worn by nearly everyone, and it stands as a time-honored symbol of Russia.

In my hat, handpainted bouclé emulates the curly texture of the Persian lamb, from which many fur hats are made. The shaping of the hat is slightly wider at the top of the crown just like those favored by the Russian Cossacks. Too nomadic? *Nyet*! It's perfect!

Cossack

The lower part of the hat is worked sideways and shaped with short rows, then sewn into a ring. Stitches for the top are picked up around the ring and worked in the round to the center top.

FINISHED SIZE: About 22 to 24" (56 to 61 cm) circumference and 4½" (11.5 cm) tall.

YARN: About 130 yd (119 m) of chunky (Bulky #5) yarn. *We used:* Mountain Colors Moguls (96% wool, 4% nylon; 65 yd [59 m]/100 g): obsidian, 130 yd (119 m). There will be enough yarn left over to make a narrow scarf.

NEEDLES: Size 10 (6 mm): set of 5 double-pointed (dpn). Adjust needle size if necessary to obtain the correct gauge.

NOTIONS: Open-ring markers (m); tapestry needle.

GAUGE: 12 sts = 4½" (11.5 cm) and 18 rows = 4" (10 cm) in garter st.

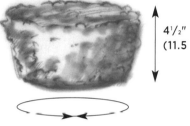

4½"
(11.5 cm)

22-24"
(56-61 cm)

SIDE RING

(Worked sideways) CO 12 sts. Work garter stitch (knit every row) until piece measures 5½" (14 cm) from CO, ending with a WS row. Turn and work short rows (see Glossary, page 136) as foll: *Short row:* (RS) *K6, wrap next st, turn, k6. Turn work to RS and place an open marker along the right selvedge of piece*. Cont in garter st (do not hide wraps) until piece measures 11" (28 cm) along side edge that does not have short rows. With RS facing, rep short row from * to *. Cont in garter st until piece measures 16½" (42 cm) from beg, measured along non-short-row edge. Rep short row from * to *. Cont in garter st until piece measures 22" (56 cm) from beg, along non-short-row edge. Rep short row from * to *. BO all sts. With yarn threaded on a tapestry needle, use a whipstitch (see Glossary, page 139) to sew BO edge to CO edge to form a ring.

CROWN TOP

With WS facing, pick up and knit 64 sts along short-rowed edge of ring (the edge with markers). Turn RS out and purl 1 row (this will not join until the next row), place an open marker (pm) in the work, and join for working in the rnd. Knit 1 rnd. Purl 1 rnd. (*Note:* Because the textured nature of the yarn makes it difficult to count stitches and rows, place an open marker in the work after each dec repeat.)

Dec rnd 1: *K6, k2tog; rep from * to end of rnd—56 sts rem.

Purl 1 rnd.

Dec rnd 2: *K5, k2tog; rep from * to end of rnd—48 sts rem.

Purl 1 rnd.

Cont dec every other rnd in this manner, knitting 1 less st between decs until 16 sts rem. *Next rnd:* *K2tog; rep from * to end of rnd—8 sts rem. Cut yarn, thread tail on a tapestry needle, draw through rem sts, and pull tight to secure.

FINISHING

Weave in loose ends.

Big Cossack

This quick-knit is a luxurious blend of a bulky singles wool and a handpainted bouclé that produces a silhouette reminiscent of the widest, but not necessarily the tallest of the Cossack fur hats.

Big Cossack

The hat is worked back and forth in rows from cuff to crown, then seamed along the center back.

FINISHED SIZE: About 22" to 24" (56 cm to 61 cm) circumference and 5½" (14 cm) tall, with brim rolled.

YARN: About 130 yd (119 m) of chunky (Bulky #5) bouclé yarn (A) and about 123 yd (112 m) of chunky (Bulky #5) smooth yarn (B).
We used: Mountain Colors Moguls (96% wool, 4% nylon; 130 yd [118 m]/200 g): moose creek (A), 130 yd (119 m). Cascade Magnum (100% wool, 123 yd [112 m]/250 g): #4006 dark brown (B), 123 yd (112 m).

NEEDLES: Cuff—Size 11 (8 mm): straight or 24" (60-cm) cir. Crown—Size 15 (10 mm): straight or 24" (60-cm) cir. Adjust needle size if necessary to obtain the correct gauge.

NOTIONS: Tapestry needle.

GAUGE: 9 sts and 14 rows = 4" (10 cm) in St st with Moguls on size 11 (8 mm) needles. 8 sts and 16 rows (8 ridges) = 4" (10 cm) in garter st with Magnum on size 15 (10 mm) needles.

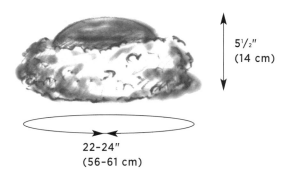

5½"
(14 cm)

22-24"
(56-61 cm)

CUFF

With A and smaller needles, CO 54 sts. Work even in St st until piece measures 10½" (26.5 cm) from beg, ending with a WS row (the purl side of cuff is the WS temporarily, until crown is finished). Cut off A, leaving a tail about 24" (61 cm) long for seaming later.

CROWN

Change to B and size 15 (10 mm) needles. *Next row:* (RS) *K4, k2tog; rep from * 9 times—45 sts rem. Mark this row as RS. Work garter st (knit every row) until crown measures 3½" (9 cm) from beg of garter st, ending with a WS row.

Dec for top as foll:

Dec row 1: (RS) *K3, k2tog; rep from * to end of row— 36 sts rem.

Knit 1 row.

Dec row 2: *K2, k2tog; rep from * to end of row—27 sts rem.

Knit 1 row.

Dec row 3: *K1, k2tog; rep from * to end of row—18 sts rem.

Knit 1 row.

Dec row 4: *K2tog; rep from * to end of row—9 sts rem.

Knit 1 row.

Cut off B, leaving a tail about 18" (45.5 cm) long for seaming. Thread tail on a tapestry needle, draw through rem loop, and pull tight to secure.

FINISHING

With B tail threaded on a tapestry needle, use invisible weaving for garter st (see Glossary, page 138) to sew crown from top of crown to brim edge. With A hanging at end of fur cuff, use invisible weaving for rev St st (see Glossary, page 138) to sew cuff seam with purl side facing (purl side will become RS of fur cuff), gently coaxing the bouclé yarn through the sts as you go. Roll cuff up 3 times so that it lies over the lower portion of the crown. With B threaded on a tapestry needle, tack cuff in place from the WS.

Velvet Pillbox

The Kazakh people are well-known for their beautiful and elaborate embroidery on all types of daily and ceremonial articles, among them the traditional Kazakh velvet vest. Scrolling floral or medallion motifs in multicolored threads are combined with beads and stones to embellish cloth, leather, felt, and other materials.

I chose a yarn of rayon chenille twisted with a wool singles in a multicolor palette that offers a rich visual surface texture in stockinette stitch. The result captures the flavor of the Kazakh embroidery on velvet in a time-honored style of the pillbox with a slightly conical crown. All in all, the hat is an easy knit that's easy to wear . . . it goes with everything!

Velvet Pillbox

This hat is worked in the round from the sides to the center top.

FINISHED SIZE: About 22" (56 cm) circumference and 2¾" (7 cm) tall.

YARN: About 140 yd (128 m) of DK-weight (Light #3) yarn. *We used:* Harrisville Designs Jasmine (100% wool twisted with rayon chenille; 70 yd [64 m]/50 g): #7176 passion flower, 140 yd (128 m).

NEEDLES: Size 5 (3.75 mm): set of 5 double-pointed (dpn). Adjust needle size if necessary to obtain the correct gauge.

NOTIONS: Marker (m); tapestry needle.

GAUGE: 19½ sts and 44 rnds = 4" (10 cm) in linen stitch patt (see Glossary, page 134, for working gauge swatches in the rnd).

STITCH GUIDE

Linen Stitch: (worked in rounds)

Rnd 1: *With yarn in back (wyb) k1, with yarn in front (wyf) sl 1 pwise; rep from * to end of rnd.

Rnd 2: *Wyf sl 1 pwise, wyb k1; rep from * to end of rnd.

Repeat Rnds 1 and 2 for pattern.

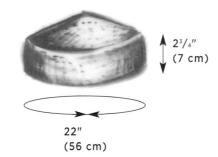

2³/₄"
(7 cm)

22"
(56 cm)

SIDES

CO 107 sts. Divide sts as evenly as possible on 4 needles, place marker (pm), and join for working in the rnd, being careful not to twist sts. Cont in linen stitch (see Stitch Guide) as foll:

Rnd 1: *Wyb k1, wyf sl 1 pwise; rep from * to last st, wyb k1.

Rnd 2: *Wyf sl 1 pwise, wyb k1; rep from * to last st, wyf sl 1 pwise.

Rep Rnds 1 and 2 until piece measures 2½" (6.5 cm) from CO. Turn work so that WS is facing, and BO all sts kwise (BO row will curl toward WS of hatband).

CROWN TOP

With yarn, RS facing and working into back loop of BO sts, pick up and knit 105 sts evenly spaced around BO edge of side band (leaving a decorative ridge on the RS), placing a marker (pm) after every 21 sts—5 sections, each containing 21 sts. Join for working in the rnd. Cont in linen st, work 1 rnd even.

Dec for top: Keeping in patt as established, work to 3 sts before first m, p3tog, work to 3 sts before second m, k3tog, cont in this manner, working p3tog before marker if the next st is a slip st or working k3tog before marker if the next st is a knit st—10 sts dec'd. Work 2 rnds even in patt. Rep the last 3 rnds 8 more times—15 sts rem. *Next rnd:* [P3tog] 5 times—5 sts rem. Cut yarn, thread tail on a tapestry needle, draw through rem sts, and pull tight to secure.

FINISHING

Weave in loose ends. Block hat using the wet towel method (see Glossary, page 130), and "hang" shaped hat on a tall, small-necked bottle to air-dry, forming a slight peak on top of crown.

Beaded Cloche

Consisting of several generations headed by the oldest man in the household, the family is the center of Afghan society. Women traditionally run the home while the men are responsible for the family's agriculture. Most Afghans live in rural villages scattered from the mountains in the north to the deserts in the south. Afghan clothing style often depends on location and ethnic group. Among traditional Afghan headdresses, many Pushtun women wear felt headdresses decorated with bits of silver, while Turkmen women decorate their headdresses with embroidery and beads.

Traditional Afghani skullcaps often had their entire surface covered with glass or metal beads embroidered with geometric patterns. An old skullcap with flat silver beads inspired my rectangular grid motif, and I've highlighted it with beads to capture the light.

Beaded Cloche

The wool/mohair blend yarn gives this hat an exquisite hand and, combined with the beads, offers a hat with some weight. This hat feels so good on, you won't want to take it off!

This hat is worked in the round from the base of the crown to the top, with beads placed along the way.

FINISHED SIZE: About 23" (58.5 cm) circumference and 7½" (19 cm) tall.

YARN: About 252 yd (230 m) each of two colors of sport-weight (Fine #2) yarn.
We used: Dale of Norway Tiur (60% mohair, 40% wool, 126 yd [115 m]/50 g): #5172 purple and #9853 lime, 252 yd (230 m) each.

NEEDLES: Size 4 (3.5 mm): 16" (40-cm) circular (cir) and set of 4 or 5 double-pointed (dpn). Adjust needle size if necessary to obtain the correct gauge.

NOTIONS: Marker (m); silver-lined size 6° seed beads (about 490 purple and 420 lime); flex beading needle(s); tapestry needle.

GAUGE: 26 sts and 26 rnds = 4" (10 cm) in charted pattern (see Glossary, page 134, for working gauge swatches in the rnd).

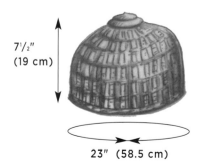

7½"
(19 cm)

23" (58.5 cm)

KNITTING WITH BEADS

To place a bead between purl sts, p1, slide bead up to sit snugly in front of this st, p1 (Figure 1).

To place a bead in front of a knit st, bring yarn to front and sl 1 purlwise (Figure 2), slide bead up to sit snugly in front of slipped st, bring yarn to back and k1 (Figure 3).

Figure 1

Figure 2

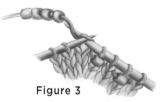

Figure 3

THREAD BEADS ONTO YARN

Using flex beading needle, thread the purple beads onto the purple yarn and the lime beads onto the lime yarn. *Note:* Wind the lime yarn into 2 balls and thread all lime beads onto one of the balls. Work Rnds 2 and 4 of Main chart with the ball containing lime beads, and Rnds 1, 3, and 5 of chart with the ball containing no beads. This will save some wear on the yarn from sliding the beads.

HAT

BORDER

With purple, CO 148 sts. Place marker (pm) and join for working in the rnd, being careful not to twist sts. Work Border chart as foll:

Rnd 1: P1 and slide a bead up close to needle, p1 without bead; rep from * to end of rnd.

Rnd 2: *P1 without bead, p1 and slide a bead up close to needle; rep from * to end of rnd.

Work Rnds 1–7 of Main chart 4 times, then work Rnds 1–5 once more—piece should measure about 5" (12.5 cm) from CO.

CROWN

Cont in patt as established, dec as foll:

Dec rnd 1: (Rnd 6 of chart) With purple, [k2, k2tog] 36 times, k4—112 sts rem.

Work Rnd 7 of chart, then work Rnds 1–5 once more.

Dec rnd 2: (Rnd 6 of chart) With purple, [k2, k2tog] 28 times—84 sts rem.

Work Rnd 7 of chart, then work Rnds 1–5 once more. Change to dpn.

Dec rnd 3: (Rnd 6 of chart) With purple, *[k2tog] 9 times, k3tog; rep from * 3 more times—40 sts rem.

Work Rnd 7, then work Rnds 1–5 once more.

Dec rnd 4: (Rnd 6 of chart) *K2tog; rep from * to end of rnd—20 sts rem.

Work Rnd 7.

Topper: With purple, purl every rnd until piece measures ¾" (2 cm) from last beaded rnd. *Next rnd:* *K2tog; rep from * to end of rnd—10 sts rem. Knit 1 rnd. Change to lime and purl 3 rnds, sliding a bead up close to needle with every st. Cut yarn, thread tail on a tapestry needle, draw through rem sts, and pull tight to secure.

FINISHING

Weave in loose ends. Spray with water to block. Let air-dry over a bowl for shape.

Border

B	·	B	·	B	·	2
·	B	·	B	·	B	1

Main

·	B	·	B	7
				6
				5
	B			4
				3
	B			2
				1

⬛ #5172 purple

· Purl on RS without bead

B Place bead as follows: P1, slide bead up to needle tip to sit snugly in front of purl st

⬜ #9853 lime - Knit on RS

B Yarn fwd, sl 1 st purlwise, slide bead to sit in front of slipped st, yarn back

◻ Pattern repeat

Pakul

This hat is the traditional wool hat of the Afghan mountain man. It's worn like a beret, and you can adjust the fit and style by rolling it from the base. The three lines of knit stitches are just the right amount of detail to spark your appreciation of the design as a whole. While the hats are usually done in a shade of camel brown, I've chosen a heathered blend of subtle lilac and gold, and you can choose from a veritable rainbow of colors. This hat looks stunning in them all. You might need several!

Pakul

This hat is worked in the round in two pieces—the sideband, which gets rolled, and the top crown. The two pieces are joined with single crochet.

FINISHED SIZE: About 23" (58.5 cm) circumference and 4" (10 cm) tall, with brim rolled.

YARN: About 396 yd (362 m) of chunky (Bulky #5) yarn. *We used:* Cascade Pastaza (50% wool, 50% llama; 132 yd [120 m]/100 g): #073 purple heather, 396 yd (362 m).

NEEDLES: Size 9 (5.5 mm): 16" (40-cm) circular (cir) and set of 4 or 5 double-pointed (dpn). Adjust needle size if necessary to obtain the correct gauge.

NOTIONS: Marker (m); tapestry needle; straight pins with colored heads; size I/9 (5.5 mm) crochet hook.

GAUGE: 16 sts and 20 rnds = 4" (10 cm) in St st worked in the rnd (see Glossary, page 134, for working gauge swatches in the rnd).

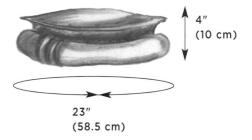

4"
(10 cm)

23"
(58.5 cm)

FINISHING

With WS tog, pin crown to side cylinder. With crochet hook, *insert hook into one st from crown and one st from sides and work 1 sc (see Glossary, page 131), joining both pieces tog; rep from * around (side cylinder and crown will match st for st) to create the prominent creased edge. Weave in loose ends. Roll sides upward to desired fit.

SIDE CYLINDER

With cir needle, CO 90 sts. Place marker (pm) and join for working in the rnd, being careful not to twist sts. *Next rnd:* [K2, p1] 3 times, knit to end of rnd. Rep this rnd until piece measures 11" (28 cm) from beg. BO all sts.

CROWN TOP

With cir needle, CO 90 sts. Pm and join for working in the rnd, being careful not to twist sts. Knit 2 rnds even. Dec for top as foll:

Dec rnd 1: [K7, k2tog] 10 times—80 sts rem.
Knit 1 rnd even.
Dec rnd 2: [K6, k2tog] 10 times—70 sts rem.
Knit 1 rnd even.
Dec rnd 3: [K5, k2tog] 10 times—60 sts rem.
Knit 1 rnd even.
Cont to dec 10 sts every other rnd in this manner, working 1 less st between decs until 20 sts rem (last dec rnd completed will be k1, k2tog). *Next rnd:* [K2tog] 10 times—10 sts rem. Cut yarn, thread tail on a tapestry needle, draw through rem sts, and pull tight to secure.

Striped Baby Hat

Pakistan historic folk costume encompasses a rich variety of both regional and tribal differences, from the northeastern borders where Hunza men wear belted shirts, khaki wool trousers, and flat rolled caps, to the Northwest Frontier Province where women may wear bright floral print dresses with embroidered pillbox hats and white head shawls. In traditional Pakistani villages, children's clothing is often just a scaled-down version of adult wear. A long shirt over baggy pants with a short vest is topped off with an embroidered pillbox. For this child's version with a softened silhouette, I've used more muted colors to capture the look of silk after it's faded to a delicate patina.

Striped Baby Hat

This hat is worked in the round from the sides to the top.

FINISHED SIZE: About 17" (43 cm) circumference and 2½" (6.5 cm) tall.

YARN: About 185 yd (169 m) each of three colors of sport-weight (Fine #2) yarn.
We used: Reynolds Saucy (100% cotton, 185 yd [169 m]/100 g): #640 periwinkle, #405 wheat, and #612 bright pink, 185 yd (169 m) each.

NEEDLES: Size 6 (4 mm): 16" (40-cm) circular (cir; optional) and set of 5 double-pointed (dpn). Adjust needle size if necessary to obtain the correct gauge.

NOTIONS: Markers (m); tapestry needle.

GAUGE: 19 sts and 32 rnds = 4" (10 cm) in reverse ridge st, worked in rnds (see Glossary, page 134, for working gauge swatches in the rnd).

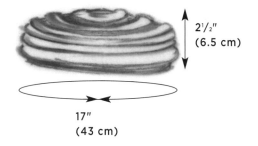

2½"
(6.5 cm)

17"
(43 cm)

CROWN SIDES

With periwinkle and cir or dpn, CO 81 sts. Divide sts as evenly as possible on 4 dpn if necessary, place marker (pm), and join for working in the rnd, being careful not to twist sts. Purl 2 rnds. Change to wheat and [knit 1 rnd, purl 2 rnds] 4 times. Change to bright pink and knit 1 rnd, purl 2 rnds. Change to periwinkle and knit 1 rnd, purl 2 rnds—piece should measure about 2½" (6.5 cm) from CO.

CROWN TOP

Change to bright pink and knit 1 rnd.
Dec rnd 1: [K7, k2tog] 9 times—72 sts rem.
Change to wheat. Knit 1 rnd.
Dec rnd 2: [K6, k2tog] 9 times—63 sts rem.
Knit 1 rnd.
Dec rnd 3: [P5, p2tog] 9 times—54 sts rem.
Purl 1 rnd.
Dec rnd 4: [K4, k2tog] 9 times—45 sts rem.
Knit 1 rnd.
Dec rnd 5: [K3, k2tog] 9 times—36 sts rem.
Change to periwinkle. Knit 1 rnd.
Dec rnd 6: [P2, p2tog] 9 times—27 sts rem.
Purl 1 rnd.
Dec rnd 7: [K1, k2tog] 9 times—18 sts rem.
Purl 1 rnd.
Dec rnd 8: [P2tog] 9 times—9 sts rem.
Cut yarn, thread tail on a tapestry needle, draw through rem sts, and pull tight to secure.

FINISHING

Weave in loose ends. Spray with water to block. Let dry over a small round biscuit tin or other sharp-edged cylindrical container to define pillbox shape.

REVERSE RIDGE STITCH

Purl 2 rnds, [knit 1 rnd, purl 2 rnds] 6 times.

Xinjiang Baby Hat

In the Xinjiang Province of northwest China, many remote minority tribes continue to favor old dress forms, accessorized with brightly colored stockings, and little hats called kolas. Bright scarves, many hand embroidered, are wrapped around the head over the kola. Tiny tots wear the little hats, too, in a palette of rich primary reds, blues, and yellows.

The motifs in this little pillbox are loosely based on Persian-style rugs from nearby Central Asia. Something about the pint-sized version of this hat just tugs at the heart.

Xinjiang Baby Hat

The sideband of this hat is worked sideways in rows, then grafted into a ring. Stitches for the top crown are picked up along one edge of the sideband ring and worked in the round to the center. The charted pattern is worked in the Fair Isle method (see Glossary, page 137), except for the spots of orange, which are worked intarsia-style (see Glossary, page 137).

FINISHED SIZE: About 20" (51 cm) circumference and 3" (7.5 cm) tall.

YARN: About 191 yd (175 m) each of five colors of fingering-weight (Super Fine #1) yarn.
We used: Dalegarn Baby Ull (100% machine washable wool; 191 yd [175 m]/50 g): #5581 navy, #4018 red, #3718 tomato red, #2908 orange, and #4227 burgundy, 191 yd (175 m) each. A few yards (meters) waste yarn for provisional cast-on.

NEEDLES: Size 1 (2.25 mm): 16" (40-cm) circular (cir) and set of 5 double-pointed (dpn). Adjust needle size if necessary to obtain the correct gauge.

NOTIONS: Stitch holder; tapestry needle; marker (m); size D/3 (3.25 mm) steel crochet hook.

GAUGE: 34 sts = 4" (10 cm) and 30 rows = 3" (7.5 cm) in St st.

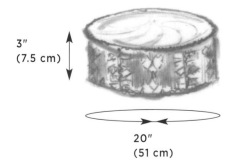

Sideband

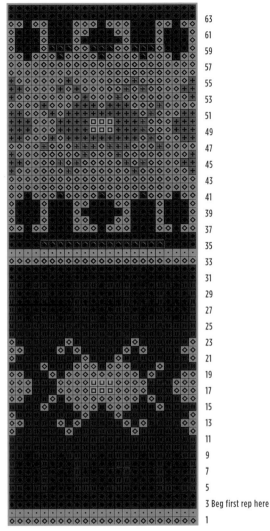

Knit on RS; purl on WS in color as shown on chart, unless otherwise indicated. Work Rows 3–64 once, then work Rows 1–64 two times.

◆ 5581 navy blue	▣ 2908 orange
· 5581 navy blue—Knit on WS	◆ 4227 burgundy red
▥ 4018 red	☐ Pattern repeat
✛ 3718 tomato red	

SIDEBAND

With navy, cir needle, and using the crochet chain method (see Glossary, page 130), provisionally CO 23 sts, leaving an 18" (45.5-cm) tail for seaming later. Do not join into a rnd. Cut navy and slide sts to opposite end of needle to begin chart on RS row. Work Rows 3–64 of Sideband chart once, then work Rows 1–64 two times—piece should measure about 20" (51 cm) from CO. Place live sts on holder. With WS facing, steam-block piece to prevent curling. Let air-dry. Remove waste yarn from provisional CO, and place live sts on one spare dpn and held sts on another spare dpn. With navy threaded on a tapestry needle, join the crown sides strip into a ring by grafting live sts tog to form garter ridge as foll: With WS tog, navy behind and burgundy in front, insert needle purlwise into first st on front needle and leave st on the needle. *Insert needle knit-wise into first st on back needle, slip st off needle, insert needle purlwise into second st on back needle and leave this st on needle. Insert needle into first st on front nee-dle knitwise, slip st off needle, insert needle purlwise into second st on front needle and leave this st on nee-dle. Rep from * until 1 st rem on each needle. Insert needle knitwise into last st on back needle and slip st off, insert needle knitwise into last st on front needle and slip st off. Weave in loose ends.

Lower edging: With orange, cir needle, and RS facing, pick up and knit 160 sts evenly spaced around left selvedge edge of crown ring, picking up between 26 and 27 sts in each of the 6 panels. Place marker (pm) and join for working in the rnd. Purl 1 rnd. Change to navy. Knit 1 rnd. BO all sts pwise. Lightly steam-block WS to help uncurl edges.

CROWN TOP

With tomato red, cir needle, and RS facing, pick up and knit 160 sts evenly spaced around other selvedge edge of crown ring. Pm and join for working in the rnd. Purl 1 rnd. Change to navy. Knit 1 rnd. Purl 1 rnd. Change to tomato red and cont as foll:

Dec rnd 1: [K14, k2tog] 10 times—150 sts rem.
Dec rnd 2: [K13, k2tog] 10 times—140 sts rem.
Knit 1 rnd even.
Dec rnd 3: [K12, k2tog] 10 times—130 sts rem.
Knit 1 rnd even.
Cont to dec 10 sts every other rnd in this manner, working 1 st fewer between decs every dec rnd until 20 sts rem. *Next rnd:* [K2tog] 10 times—10 sts rem. Cut yarn, thread tail on a tapestry needle, draw through rem sts, and pull tight to secure.

FINISHING

Steam-block lightly as follows: Turn hat inside out and lay crown as flat as possible over end of ironing board. Lightly touch iron to back of work, being careful not to flatten sts. Turn hat RS out and place over a biscuit tin or 20" (51-cm) diameter cylinder. Spray with water. Let air-dry completely.

Knot-Topped Calotte

A deep black skullcap, the calotte is one of the most common type of headpiece worn by Chinese men. It has a wide lower band, with a crown sectioned in four to six triangular shapes designed to hug the head. Its only distinguishing feature is a colorful cord knot placed on top for identification and good luck. Knots were used in ancient times to record events, and eventually knotting evolved into a decorative art for use on clothing and jewelry. I have knot-topped this calotte with a pale gold, over a hat of light magenta, a luscious color used frequently in Chinese silks.

Knot-Topped Calotte

This hat is worked in the round from the base to the crown, and finished off with a knitted cord top-knot.

FINISHED SIZE: About 23" (58.5 cm) circumference and 7½" (19 cm) tall, excluding top-knot.

YARN: About 218 yd (199 m) of main color and 109 yd (100 m) of contrast color in sport-weight (Fine #2) yarn. *We used:* Cascade Pima Silk (85% pima cotton, 15% silk; 109 yd [100 m]/50 g): magenta, 218 yd (199 m); light gold, 109 yd (100 m).

NEEDLES: Size 4 (3.5 mm): 16" (40-cm) circular (cir) and set of 4 or 5 double-pointed (dpn). Spare cir needle the same size or smaller.

NOTIONS: A few yards (meters) waste yarn for provisional cast-on; marker (m); removable marker; size F/5 (3.75 mm) crochet hook; tapestry needle.

GAUGE: 23½ sts and 32 rnds = 4" (10 cm) in St st worked in the rnd (see Glossary, page 134, for working gauge swatches in the rnd).

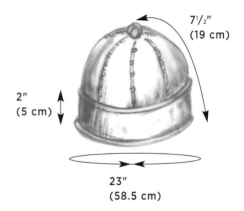

7½"
(19 cm)

2"
(5 cm)

23"
(58.5 cm)

FACING

With waste yarn and magenta, and using the crochet chain method (see Glossary, page 130), provisionally CO 138 sts. Place marker (pm) and join for working in the rnd, being careful not to twist sts. Work St st (knit every rnd) until piece measures 2" (5 cm) from beg.

BRIM

Change to light gold. Knit 1 rnd. Purl 3 rnds. Change to magenta and work the light gold rows into a "corded" edge as foll: Fold light gold section with WS tog, insert right needle tip into first light gold st on left needle then into first light gold purl bump on WS of corresponding st 4 rows below needle, and knit these 2 sts tog. Working each st on needle with the corresponding purl bump 4 rows below, join sts tog to end of rnd. Cont with magenta, knit even until piece measures 2" (5 cm) from cording row. Remove provisional yarn from CO and place live facing sts on spare cir needle. Fold facing to WS. Change to light gold. Join facing to hat as foll: *K1 from front needle tog with 1 st from facing needle; rep from * (do not BO) to end of rnd—138 sts rem. Cont with light gold, purl 2 rnds. Change to magenta and work even in St st until piece measures 4¾" (12 cm) from the light gold cording row at lower brim edge.

CROWN

Rnd 1: With magenta, *k20, work vertical double decrease (sl 2 tog kwise, k1, p2sso; see Glossary, page 133); rep from * to end of rnd—12 sts dec'd; 126 sts rem.

Rnd 2 and all even-numbered rnds: Knit to end of rnd, remove m, k1 of next rnd, replace m—the first st of previous rnd becomes last st of this rnd.

Rnd 3: *K18, work vertical double dec; rep from * to end of rnd—114 sts rem.

Rnd 5: *K16, work vertical double dec; rep from * to end of rnd—102 sts rem.

Rnd 7: *K14, work vertical double dec; rep from * to end of rnd—90 sts rem.

Rnd 9: *K12, work vertical double dec; rep from * to end of rnd—78 sts rem.

Rnd 11: *K10, work vertical double dec; rep from * to end of rnd—66 sts rem.

Rnd 13: *K8, work vertical double dec; rep from * to end of rnd—54 sts rem.

Rnd 15: *K6, work vertical double dec; rep from * to end of rnd—42 sts rem.

Rnd 17: *K4, work vertical double dec; rep from * to end of rnd—30 sts rem.

Rnd 19: *K2, work vertical double dec; rep from * to end of rnd—18 sts rem.

Rnd 21: *Work vertical double dec; rep from * to end of rnd—6 sts rem.

Cut yarn, thread tail on a tapestry needle, draw through rem sts, and pull tight to secure.

FINISHING

Couching: Beg at crown top and working from center st of vertical double dec, follow the vertical line of dec sts down to the first St st rnd just above the upper edge of light gold border. Mark this st. Thread tapestry needle with 24" (61-cm) length of light gold, *bring needle up from WS of work on the left side of marked st, then down to WS at the right side edge of the same st so that the light gold couching sts will lie horizontally across this vertical line of magenta sts. Do not tighten yarn, but leave a small space beneath the light gold st to later thread the light gold strands that will lay over the magenta knitted

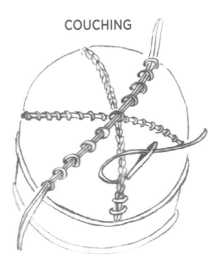

COUCHING

surface. Rep from * every 3 or 4 rows up, covering another vertical double dec st (see couching illustration at
right), rethreading needle as necessary. Work from the
upper light gold edge of the hat, over the top of the
crown and down the opposite side of crown to the
upper light gold edge. Rep the horizontal couching sts
along each of the dec lines (6 lines total). Cut 3 strands
of light gold, each 15" (38 cm) long. Thread all 3
strands on a tapestry needle and thread them under
each of the prepared couching stitches, working from
the upper light gold brim edge to the opposite upper
light gold brim edge, pulling strands snug, but not so
tight as to pucker the hat. Tighten couching sts over
strands. Weave in loose ends.

Chinese knot: With light gold and dpn, CO 3 sts. Work
3-st knitted cord (see Glossary, page 137) until piece
measures 5" (12.5 cm) from beg. K3tog—1 st rem. Cut
yarn, and pull tail through rem st to fasten off.
Following Figures 1 and 2 at right, twist cord into
double-coin knot, pulling gently to form a round "ball."
Thread tail end of cord on tapestry needle and insert to
WS on one side of intersection at top. Rep for other tail
of cord to center knot on top of hat. Tie the two tails
into a square knot on inside of hat. Weave in loose
ends. Spray with water outside and inside to block and
set sts. Place hat over a bowl and let air-dry.

CHINESE KNOT

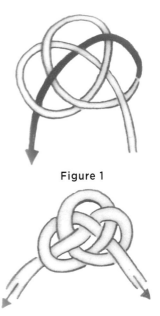

Figure 1

Figure 2

THAILAND

Folded Bloom

Sa wat dee! Maintaining tradition and delighting the eye, the hill tribes of northern Thailand greet each other wearing colorful handwoven and heavily embroidered daily costume. The intense, saturated color of striped fabrics and a Thai hat that resembles a folded bloom were my inspirations for this tasseled pillbox. The linen's rich texture provides a lovely drape in the folds and a firm stability in the sculptural sides. This hat transforms a flat piece of knitted fabric into a showcase of folds.

Folded Bloom

The crown top is worked sideways in rows and sewn into a ring, then stitches for the sides are picked up from the ring and worked downwards in the round.

FINISHED SIZE: About 22½" (57 cm) circumference and 7" (18 cm) tall.

YARN: About 135 yd (123 m) each of four colors of sport-weight (Fine #2) yarn.
We used: Euroflax Originals (100% linen; 135 yd [123 m]/50 g) #18.20 emerald, #18.45 violet, #18.35 mustard, and #18.27 crabapple blossom (pink), 135 yd (123 m) each.

NEEDLES: Size 3 (3.25 mm): 16" (40-cm) circular (cir), another cir needle same length but 1 or 2 sizes smaller to use as spare. Size 5 (3.75 mm): set of 4 or 5 double-pointed (dpn). Adjust needle size if necessary to obtain the correct gauge.

NOTIONS: Size D/3 (3.25 mm) crochet hook; marker (m); tapestry needle; 2" (5-cm) square of cardboard for making pom-pom.

GAUGE: 23 sts = 4" (10 cm) and 8 ridges (16 rows) = 1" (2.5 cm) in garter st on size 3 (3.25 mm) needles.

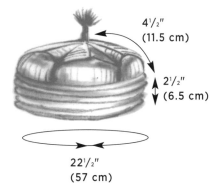

4½"
(11.5 cm)

2½"
(6.5 cm)

22½"
(57 cm)

ASSEMBLY

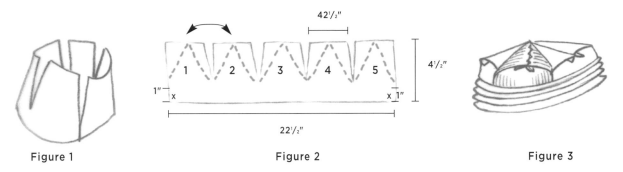

| Figure 1 | Figure 2 | Figure 3 |

CROWN

With emerald and size 3 (3.25 mm) cir needle, CO 25 sts. *Set-up row*: (WS) Knit. Working color progression in garter st (knit every row), work Rows 1–72 of Crown chart (see page 116) 4 times (binding off 17 sts at beg of Row 70 each time, then using the cable method [see Glossary, page 130] to CO 17 sts at beg of Row 72). Then work Rows 1–69 once more. *Next row:* (Row 70 of chart) BO all sts—5 sections completed. With emerald, crochet hook, and holding RS tog, work slip st crochet (see Glossary, page 132) to join short edges of strip tog for 1" (2.5 cm) from lower edge as shown in Figure 1.

SIDES

With pink, RS facing, and size 3 (3.25 mm) cir needle, pick up and knit 26 sts in each section along lower edge of crown—130 sts total. Place marker (pm) and join for working in the rnd. Purl 1 rnd. Knit 6 rnds.
Outer ridges: With WS facing, use spare smaller cir needle to pick up the back loop of each st along the pick-up row. Fold work with WS tog so that needles are parallel and join the sts by working 1 st from each needle tog as k2tog, connecting the sts together and forcing the fold to project sculpturally on the RS of work. Purl 1 rnd. Change to emerald. *Knit 6 rnds. With spare smaller cir needle, pick up back loops of previous

color at color change. Fold work with WS tog and work 1 st from each needle tog as k2tog. Purl 1 rnd. Change to violet and rep from *. Work 6 more bands in the same manner, 1 each in the foll colors: pink, emerald, mustard, violet, emerald, pink—9 bands total. BO all sts on the purl rnd foll the last pink band.

FINISHING

Fold crown: Mark mid-point on upper edge of each of the 5 crown sections as shown in Figure 2. With WS tog, fold Section 1 and 2 tog. With violet threaded on a tapestry needle and using a backstitch (see Glossary, page 138), sew along dashed line as shown in figure. Fold rem half of Section 2 with Section 3, and backstitch along dashed line. Fold rem half of Section 3 with Section 4, and backstitch along dashed line. Fold rem half of Section 4 with Section 5, and backstitch along dashed line. Fold rem half of Section 5 with Section 1, and backstitch along dashed line. Steam-block lightly, using your fingers to press seams open. The WS of crown piece will fold to the RS of the hat.
Join rem section seams: Where 2 sections meet at top of crown, fold under the excess fabric so that the pieces fit the crown, folding under about ½" (1.3 cm) at outer edge and tapering to about ⅛" (3 mm) at the top of the crown (Figure 3). With violet and using the invisible weaving for garter st method (see Glossary, page 138)

Crown

Cable CO 17 sts, knit 25 sts to end.

BO 17 sts beg of WS row, knit to end.

- ⊡ Knit on WS using color as shown on chart
- ◈ #18.20 emerald—Knit on RS
- ▲ #18.45 violet—Knit on RS
- ‖ #18.35 mustard—Knit on RS
- ✛ #18.27 crabapple blossom (pink)—Knit on RS
- ☐ No stitch
- ⌒ Bind off
- ☐ Pattern repeat

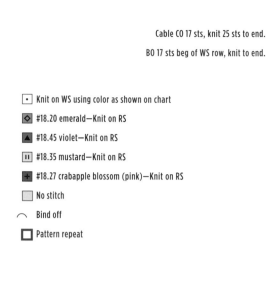

K8 sts, turn work.

and working toward the top of the crown, sew seam. *Note:* Colors will not match at this seam. Rep for other sections.

Top cord: With 2 strands of pink held tog and dpn, CO 4 sts. Work 4-st knitted cord until piece measures 1¼" (3.2 cm) from beg. [K2tog] 2 times—2 sts rem. Cut yarn, leaving 10" (25.5-cm) tails. Draw tails through rem 2 sts and pull tight to secure.

Pom-pom: Wind 2 strands of pink around a 2" (5-cm) piece of cardboard about 25 times. Slide strands off cardboard and use the two 10" (25.5 cm) yarn tails from the top cord to tie the center of this group to the end of the cord in a tight square knot. Cut loops, shake out pom-pom, and trim even if necessary. Using a whipstitch (see Glossary, page 139), sew cord tightly to top of crown so that it stands vertically.

Work rows 1–72 four times, then Rows 1–69 and BO all sts on Row 70 (5 sections complete).

Dancer's Hat

Dance has always been an integral part of Japanese culture, whether one watches or participates. Early dances expressed the need to revere a god or spirit, celebrate a good harvest, pray for a good catch, or exorcise evil spirits. To this day, Japanese folk dances are performed at festivals and special occasions.

Since bright colors always feature prominently in the costumes for these dances, I have chosen the intense and saturated colors of red and blue in a yarn with a silk-like sheen, and I've edged the leaf shapes with bright marigold. This sculptural affair will be a real conversation showpiece.

Dancer's Hat

This hat is worked in the round from the base to the top. The decorative leaves are worked separately (back and forth in rows), then sewn to the hat, and topped off with a "gumdrop" point.

FINISHED SIZE: About 23½" (59.5 cm) circumference and 6½" (16.5 cm) tall, excluding gumdrop.

YARN: About 218 yd (199 m) of main color and 109 yd (100 m) each of two contrasting colors of sport-weight (Fine #2) yarn.
We used: Cascade Pima Tencel (50% pima cotton, 50% tencel; 109 yd [100 m]/50 g): #7478 red, 218 yd (199 m); #1694 blue and #3183 orange, 109 yd (100 m) each.

NEEDLES: Size 4 (3.5 mm): 16" (40-cm) circular (cir) and set of 4 or 5 double-pointed (dpn). Adjust needle size if necessary to obtain the correct gauge.

NOTIONS: Marker (m); tapestry needle; small amount of polyester fiberfill (or a cotton ball) to stuff top gumdrop; long sewing pins with large colored heads.

GAUGE: 23 sts and 28 rnds = 4" (10 cm) in St st worked in the rnd.

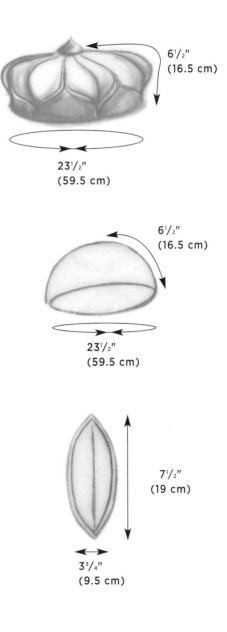

HAT

With blue and cir needle, CO 134 sts. Place marker (pm) and join for working in the rnd, being careful not to twist sts. Work k1, p1 rib for 2 rnds. Change to St st (knit every rnd), inc 1 st at beg of first rnd—135 sts. Work even in St st until piece measures 4" (10 cm) from CO.

Dec for top:

Rnd 1: *K7, k2tog; rep from * to end of rnd—120 sts rem.

Rnd 2 and all even-numbered rnds: Knit.

Rnd 3: *K6, k2tog; rep from * to end of rnd—105 sts rem.

Rnd 5: *K5, k2tog; rep from * to end of rnd—90 sts rem.

Cont in this manner, dec 15 sts every other rnd and working 1 st fewer between decs on dec rnds until 30 sts rem. *Next rnd:* *K2tog; rep from * to end of rnd—15 sts rem. Cut yarn, thread tail on a tapestry needle, draw through rem sts, and pull tight to secure.

LEAF (MAKE 6)

Note: Use the backward loop CO (see Glossary, page 130) for all increases (inc 1).

With red, CO 3 sts. Purl 1 WS row. Inc as foll:

Row 1: (RS) K1, inc 1, sl 1 kwise (center st), inc 1, k1—5 sts.

Row 2: K1, p3, k1.

Row 3: K1, p1, inc 1, sl 1 kwise, inc 1, p1, k1—7 sts.

Row 4: [K1, p1] 3 times, k1.

Row 5: K1, p1, k1, inc 1, sl 1 kwise, inc 1, k1, p1, k1—9 sts.

Rows 6, 8, 10, 12, 14, 16, and 18: K1, p1, k1, purl to last 3 sts, k1, p1, k1.

Row 7: K1, p1, k2, inc 1, sl 1 kwise, inc 1, k2, p1, k1—11 sts.

Row 9: K1, p1, k3, inc 1, sl 1 kwise, inc 1, k3, p1, k1—13 sts.

Row 11: K1, p1, k4, inc 1, sl 1 kwise, inc 1, k4, p1, k1—15 sts.

Row 13: K1, p1, k5, inc 1, sl 1 kwise, inc 1, k5, p1, k1—17 sts.

Row 15: K1, p1, k6, inc 1, sl 1 kwise, inc 1, k6, p1, k1—19 sts.

Row 17: K1, p1, k7, inc 1, sl 1 kwise, inc 1, k7, p1, k1—21 sts.

Row 19: K1, p1, k8, sl 1 kwise, k8, p1, k1.

Row 20: K1, p1, k1, p15, k1, p1, k1.

Rep Rows 19 and 20 until piece measures 5½" (14 cm) from CO. Dec as foll:

Row 1: K1, p1, knit to 1 st before slipped center st, work vertical double dec (sl 2 sts tog kwise, k1, p2sso; see Glossary, page 133), knit to last 2 sts, p1, k1—19 sts rem.

Row 2 and all even-numbered rows: K1, p1, k1, purl to last 3 sts, k1, p1, k1.

Row 3: Rep Row 1—17 sts rem.

Rep Rows 2 and 3, keeping continuity of seed st edges and working vertical double decrease every other row until 5 sts rem, ending with a WS row as foll: k1, p3, k1. *Next row:* (RS) K1, work vertical double dec, k1—3 sts rem. *Next row:* P3tog—1 st rem. Cut yarn, draw tail through rem st, and pull tight to secure.

Border: With orange and RS facing, pick up and knit 4 sts for every 5 rows along one side of leaf. BO all sts evenly, being careful not to BO too tight (use a larger needle if necessary). Rep for other side of leaf. Thread orange tail on tapestry needle and connect orange borders invisibly at each leaf tip. Weave in loose ends. Steam-block each leaf and let dry completely before handling.

FINISHING

Attach leaves: Using long sewing pins, mark 6 points evenly spaced around lower edge of hat. Center the CO point (this will be the lower CO leaf edge) of one leaf at each of these 6 points, aligning them with the lower edge of hat, and pin in place. Pin the opposite end (the p3tog end) of each leaf at top of crown. Place another pin in each leaf 2" (5 cm) up from base of crown. Working one leaf at a time, remove pin at base of leaf and fold leaf tip back to the 2" (5 cm) pin mark, with WS showing and red threaded on a tapestry needle, sew center of leaf (along slipped st "stem") to hat by inserting tapestry needle under a hat st close to the fold, then under 1 or 2 purl bars on WS of leaf, ending with CO point of leaf at base of hat. The leaf tip will roll in direction of the seam as you sew. Work a whipstitch over last seam stitch to secure thread. Weave in end on WS of leaf, thus keeping inside of crown tidy. Rep seam process for the upper 2" (5 cm) of each leaf, working toward top of cap crown.

Gumdrop: With orange and dpn, CO 21 sts. Divide sts evenly on 3 dpn. Pm and join for working in the rnd, being careful not to twist sts. Purl 3 rnds. Change to blue. Knit 1 rnd. Dec as foll:

Dec rnd 1: *K4, work vertical double dec; rep from * to end of rnd—15 sts rem. Knit 2 rnds even. Remove m, knit first st of next rnd onto last needle, replace m (beg of rnd is moved forward by 1 st). Rotate sts so that there are 5 sts on each of 3 dpn.

Dec rnd 2: *K2, work vertical double dec; rep from * to end of rnd—9 sts rem.

Knit 2 rnds even. Remove m, knit first st of next rnd onto last needle, replace m (beg of rnd is moved forward by 1 st). Rotate sts so that there are 3 sts on each of 3 dpn.

Dec rnd 3: *Work vertical double dec; rep from * to end of rnd—3 sts rem.

Cut yarn, thread tail on a tapestry needle, draw through rem sts, and pull tight to secure into a point. Stuff gumdrop lightly with fiberfill (or cotton ball). With orange, sew gumdrop to top of hat.

Samurai Kabuto

As the hereditary warrior class in feudal Japan, samurai often engaged in hand-to-hand combat on the battlefield. The winner of an engagement would decapitate his opponent and keep the head as a trophy. This brutal ritual gave rise to the heavy protective nature of the samurai helmet. The crown, the visor, the neck protector, the side wings, and the symbolic regalia adorning the front crown all worked together to protect the samurai and promote a ferocious appearance.

I've used linen in a combination of ribbing and button stitch to mimic the heavy decorative cord and metal construction of a samurai neck protector; the palette mimics the patina of metal. The dragon on the front crown of my helmet serves as the warrior's crest.

Samurai Kabuto

The crown of this hat is worked in rounds from the bottom to the top. The neck protector and brim are worked separately in rows, then sewn to the crown. The top of the hat is decorated with a knitted cord tassel and a three-dimensional embroidered, beaded dragon. Most of the hat is worked with two strands of yarn held together.

FINISHED SIZE: About 22½" (57 cm) circumference, 7" (18 cm) high along black crown, and 12½" (31.5 cm) long from top of crown to bottom of neck piece.

YARN: About 270 yd (247 m) each of two colors and 135 yd (123 m) each of two other colors of sport-weight (Fine #2) yarn. *We used:* Euroflax Originals (100% linen; 135 yd [123 m]/ 50 g): #18.22 black and #18.02 ginger, 270 yd (247 m) each; #18.35 mustard and #18.46 mahogany, 135 yd (123 m) each.

NEEDLES: Size 4 (3.5 mm): 16" (40-cm) and 24" (60-cm) circular (cir) and set of 4 double-pointed (dpn). Size 3 (3.25 mm): set of 4 dpn. Size 1 (2.25 mm): straight or cir. Adjust needle size if necessary to obtain the correct gauge.

NOTIONS: Size 3 (2.1 mm) steel crochet hook; markers (m); tapestry needle; small amount of polyester fiberfill to stuff dragon; about 50 size 6° round brown silver-lined seed beads to embellish couching; sharp-point sewing needle; beeswax (for strengthening sewing thread); two ¼" (6-mm) oval-shaped beads for dragon eyes; two 1⅛" (3-cm) black smooth-surface shank buttons.

GAUGE: Crown: 20 sts and 30 rnds = 4" (10 cm) in sl st knit rib st on larger needles with 2 strands held tog. Neck protector/wings: 26 sts and 24 rows = 4" (10 cm) in k1, p1 rib and button stitch combo on larger needles with 2 strands held tog. 6 sts and 8 rows = 1" (2.5 cm) in St st on size 1 (2.25 mm) needles with a single strand of yarn.

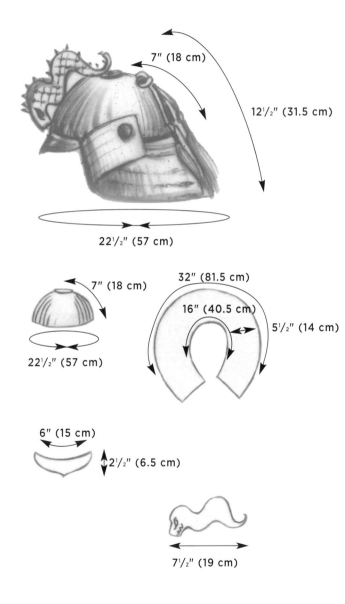

7" (18 cm)

12½" (31.5 cm)

22½" (57 cm)

7" (18 cm)

22½" (57 cm)

32" (81.5 cm)

16" (40.5 cm)

5½" (14 cm)

6" (15 cm)

2½" (6.5 cm)

7½" (19 cm)

STITCH GUIDE

Button Stitch: (worked over 2 sts)
*Bring right needle in front of next 2 sts on left needle and insert right needle tip between the second and third sts on left needle. Wrap working yarn around right needle, draw up a loop, slip this loop pwise onto left needle tip, and knit it through the back loop (1 new st on right needle), slip right needle into the 2 wrapped sts on left needle (these are the first and second sts on left needle), then slip them pwise to right needle, then pass the new st on right needle over the top of the 2 sts slipped sts and off needle; rep from * as directed for each button stitch.

Seed Stitch: (odd number of sts)
Row 1: *K1, p1; rep from * to last st, k1.
Repeat Row 1 for pattern.

Slip Stitch Knit Rib: (worked in rnds)
Rnd 1: *K2, sl 1; rep from * to end of rnd.
Rnd 2: Knit.
Repeat Rnds 1 and 2 for pattern.

CROWN

With 2 strands of black held tog and longer size 4 (3.5-mm) cir needle, CO 108 sts. Place marker (pm) and join for working in the rnd, being careful not to twist sts. Work slip st knit rib as foll:
Rnd 1: *K2, sl 1; rep from * to end of rnd.
Rnd 2: Knit.
Rnds 3–42: Rep Rnds 1 and 2—piece should measure about 5½" (14 cm) from CO after Rnd 42.
Rnd 43: *K2tog, sl 1; rep from * to end of rnd—72 sts rem.
Rnd 44: Knit.
Rnd 45: *K1, sl 1; rep from * to end of rnd.
Rnd 46: Knit—piece should measure about 6" (15 cm) from CO (if not, cont to rep Rnds 45 and 46 as necessary).
Rnd 47: *K2tog; rep from * to end of rnd—36 sts rem.
Rnd 48: Rep Rnd 47—18 sts rem. Drop yarn but do not cut. Change to 2 strands of mustard held tog. Knit 1 rnd. Purl 1 rnd. Cut mustard. Pick up black, knit 1 rnd, purl 1 rnd. *Next rnd:* *P1, p2tog; rep from * to end of rnd—12 sts rem. *Next rnd:* *P2tog; rep from * to end of rnd—6 sts rem. Cut yarn, thread tail on a tapestry needle, draw through rem sts, and pull tight to secure.

NECK PROTECTOR/WINGS

Note: Use the backward loop CO (see Glossary, page 130) for all increases (inc 1).
With 2 strands of ginger and longer size 4 (3.5 mm) cir needle, CO 186 sts. *First row:* (WS) *K1, p1; rep from * to end of row. Work 2 more rows in rib as established. Do not cut off yarn. Change to mustard. *Button st row:* (RS) K1, *work button st (see Stitch Guide) around next 2 sts; rep from * to last st, k1. Cut mustard. Slide all sts to other end of needle, pick up ginger yarn still

attached, and work another RS row as foll: K43, pm, k4, [inc 1, k10] 9 times, inc 1, k6, pm, k43—196 sts. Beg with WS row, work k1, p1 rib for 3 rows, ending with a WS row completed. With RS facing, rejoin mustard and rep button st row. Slide sts to other end of needle, pick up ginger yarn still attached, and work another RS row as foll: Knit to first m, slip m (sl m), k4, [inc 1, k11] 9 times, inc 1, k7, sl m, knit to end—206 sts. Beg with WS row, work k1, p1 rib for 5 rows. Pick up mustard and rep button st row. Slide sts to other end of needle, pick up ginger yarn still attached, knit to first m, sl m, k6, [inc 1, k12] 9 times, inc 1, k6, sl m, knit to end—216 sts. Beg with WS row, work k1, p1 rib for 5 rows. Pick up mustard and rep button st row. Slide sts to other end of needle, pick up ginger yarn still attached, knit to first m, sl m, k6, [inc 1, k13] 9 times, inc 1, k7, sl m, knit to end—226 sts. Beg with WS row, work k1, p1 rib for 5 rows. Pick up mustard and rep button st row. Slide sts to other end of needle, pick up ginger yarn still attached, knit to first m, sl m, k7, [inc 1, k14] 9 times, inc 1, k7, sl m, knit to end—236 sts. Beg with WS row, work k1, p1 rib for 7 rows. Pick up mustard and rep button st row. Slide sts to other end of needle, pick up ginger yarn still attached, and BO all sts in ribbing. Lay flat and lightly steam any rippling edges. Let air-dry completely.

BRIM

With 2 strands mahogany and size 4 (3.5 mm) needles, CO 27 sts. Work seed st (see Stitch Guide) until piece measures 1" (2.5 cm) from beg. P2tog at beg of next 2 rows—25 sts rem. K2tog at beg of next 2 rows—23 sts rem. BO 7 sts at beg of next 2 rows, slipping first st in row to make a smooth curve—9 sts rem. BO 2 sts at beg of next 2 rows, also slipping first st for a smooth curve—5 sts rem. BO 1 st at beg of next 2 rows, also slipping

first st—3 sts rem. Sl 1, k2tog, psso—1 st rem. Cut yarn, draw tail through rem st, and pull tight to secure.

FINISHING

Cord and tassel: With 2 strands of mahogany held tog and size 3 (3.25 mm) dpn, CO 3 sts, leaving 8" (20.5-cm) tails for later finishing. Work 3-st knitted cord (see Glossary, page 137) until piece measures 11" (28 cm) from beg. *Next row:* Sl 1, k2tog, psso—1 st rem. Cut yarn, leaving 8" (20.5-cm) tails, and draw tails through last loop to secure. *Cut 20 strands of mahogany, each 14" (35.5 cm) long for the tassel. Spread out one pair of 8" (20.5-cm) knitted cord tails on a flat surface. Place the 20 tassel strands perpendicular to and centered between the tails. Use the tails to tie a square knot at the halfway point of the 14" (35.5-cm) tassel strands. Rep from * to make a tassel on the other end of the knitted cord.

Tassel wrap: Cut 2 strands of mustard, each about 12" (30.5 cm) long. Beg about 1¼" (3.2 cm) down from top of tassel, wrap mustard strands around the tassel head (see Glossary, page 134) for about ¾" (2 cm). Fasten off.

Dragon: Dragon is worked with a single strand of yarn on size 1 (2.25 mm) needle. The entire bottom section (belly, etc.) of dragon is worked in garter st, beginning at the nose.

Bottom section: With a single strand of mahogany and size 1 (2.25 mm) needle, CO 2 sts. Work even in garter st until piece measures 1" (2.5 cm) from CO. *Inc row:* K1f&b (see Glossary, page 135), knit to end of row—1 st inc'd. Rep inc row 5 more times—8 sts. Cont in garter st until piece measures 3" (7.5 cm) from CO. Dec 1 st (k2tog) at beg of next 2 rows—6 sts rem. Work even until piece measures 5" (12.5 cm) from CO. K2tog at beg of next 2 rows—4 sts rem. Work even until piece measures 6½" (16.5 cm) from CO. *Next row:* [K2tog] 2 times—2 sts rem. Work even until piece measures

8" (20.5 cm) from CO. K2tog—1 st rem. Cut yarn,
thread tail through rem st, and pull tight to secure.
Left side body: With a single strand of mustard and
size 1 (2.25 mm) needle, CO 64 sts. Purl 1 row. Cont as
foll, using the backward CO method for all increases
(inc 1):

Row 1: (RS) [K2tog, k1] 3 times, k10, [k2tog] 3 times,
place marker (pm), k25, [inc 1, k1] 5 times, pm,
k9—63 sts rem.

Row 2: P9, slip marker (sl m), p10, [p2tog, p1] 5 times,
p10, sl m, p10, [p2tog, p1] 3 times—55 sts rem.

Row 3: Sl 1, k2tog, psso, [k2tog, pass previous st over
dec'd st] 3 times, [k1, k2tog] 2 times, k1, sl m, [k1,
inc 1] 5 times, k5, [k2tog] 5 times, k10, sl m, [k1, inc 1]
2 times, k7—47 sts rem.

Row 4: Purl to last st (do not work last st), turn work.

Row 5: Sl 1 (2 sts on right needle), pass last unworked st
from previous row over the slipped st, k2tog, pass
previous st over dec'd st, k2, sl m, [k1, inc 1] 7
times, k5, [k2tog, k1] 3 times, [k1, inc 1] 5 times, k4,
sl m, k11—53 sts rem.

Row 6: Purl to last st (do not work last st), turn work.

Row 7: Sl 1 (2 sts on right needle), pass last unworked st
from previous row over the slipped st, k1, sl m, k18,
[k2tog] 3 times, k15, sl m, [k1, inc 1] 3 times, k8—
52 sts.

Row 8: BO 6 sts, purl to m, sl m, purl to end—46 sts
rem.

Row 9: Sl 1, k1, psso, remove m, k1, BO 1 st, knit to
end—44 sts rem.

Row 10: Slipping first st, BO 7 sts, remove m, purl to
end—37 sts.

Row 11: Sl 1, k1, psso, [k2, inc 1] 6 times, k1, [k2tog] 3
times, k3, [k1, inc 1] 9 times, k3 (1 st unworked),
turn—48 sts.

Row 12: Sl 1 (2 sts on right needle), pass last unworked
st from previous row over the slipped st, purl to end
of row—47 sts.

Row 13: Slipping first st, BO all sts.

Right side body: With single strand of mustard and size 1
(2.25 mm) needle, CO 64 sts. Purl 1 row. Cont as foll,
using the backward loop CO for all increases (inc 1):

Row 1: (RS) K9, pm, [k1, inc 1] 5 times, k25, pm, [k2tog]
3 times, k10, [k2tog, k1] 3 times—63 sts rem.

Row 2: [P2tog, p1] 3 times, p10, sl m, p10, [p2tog, p1] 5
times, p10, sl m, p9—55 sts rem.

Row 3: K7, [k1, inc 1] 2 times, sl m, k10, [k2tog] 5 times,
k5, [k1, inc 1] 5 times, sl m, k1, [k1, k2tog] 2 times,
[k2tog] 4 times, k1—51 sts rem.

Row 4: Slipping first st, BO 4 sts purlwise, purl to end of
row—47 sts rem.

Row 5: K11, sl m, k4, [k1, inc 1] 5 times, [k2tog, k1] 3
times, k5, [k1, inc 1] 7 times, sl m, k2, k2tog, k1 (1 st
unworked), turn—55 sts.

Row 6: Sl 1 (2 sts on right needle) pass last unworked st
from previous row over the slipped st, p1, psso, purl
to end—53 sts rem.

Row 7: K8, [k1, inc 1] 3 times, sl m, k15, [k2tog] 3 times,
k18, sl m, k2 (1 st unworked), turn.

Row 8: Sl 1 (2 sts on right needle), pass last unworked st
from previous row over the slipped st, p1, psso, purl
to end of row—51 sts rem.

Row 9: Slipping first st, BO 6 sts kwise, knit to last st (1 st
unworked), turn—45 sts rem.

Row 10: Remove m, sl 1 (2 sts on right needle), pass last
unworked st from previous row over the slipped st,
p1, psso, purl to last st (1 st unworked), turn—43 sts
rem.

Row 11: Sl 1 (2 sts on right needle), pass last unworked
st from previous row over the slipped st, BO 6 more
sts knitwise, knit to end of row—36 sts rem.

Row 12: Sl 1, p1, psso, [p2, inc 1] 6 times, p1, [p2tog] 3 times, p3, [p1, inc 1] 9 times, p2, (1 st unworked), turn—47 sts.

Row 13: Sl 1 (2 sts on right needle), remove m, pass last unworked st of previous row over the slipped st, knit to last st (1 st unworked), turn—46 sts rem.

Row 14: Sl 1 (2 sts on right needle), pass last unworked st from previous row over the slipped st, BO all sts purlwise to end of row.

FINISHING

Weave in all loose ends. Steam-press each dragon side body (you may touch the iron to the knitted surface). Lightly steam dragon bottom body, but do not touch iron to the knitting. Let dry completely.

Couching: (see Glossary, page 133) With a single strand of ginger, lay couching grid on dragon according to Figure 1 on page 127, each parallel line spaced about ½" (1.3 cm) apart on each dragon side body. Cut a length of sewing thread and draw through a disk of beeswax to coat. "Press" the thread by *quickly* pulling it under a hot iron. With sewing needle and waxed thread, secure couching intersections with beads as foll: Insert sewing needle up from WS at point #1, through bead, down to WS at point #2, up at point #3, through bead, and down at point #4.

Face: With single strand of mahogany threaded on a tapestry needle, work eyebrow in stem stitch (see Glossary, page 134). Sew on large bead for eye and small bead for nostril. Steam lightly to set, let dry.

Assembly: With a single strand of mahogany and using a whipstitch (see Glossary, page 139), sew each side body lower edge (solid line a on Figure 1) to edge (a) of dragon bottom body (Figure 2). With WS tog, pin nose, head, and first back curve (dotted line b) of each side body tog. With single strand of ginger and crochet hook, work single crochet (sc; see Glossary, page 131)

from right to left across nose (see Figure 2), beg at (c) and work to (d). Then crochet along nose/head from (d) to (e) as foll: *Ch 5, sc in next 2 sts; rep from * to (e). Insert a bit of fiberfill into the nose/head to shape the head. Cont along back curves from (e) to (f) as foll: *Ch 7, sc in next 2 sts; rep from *, and inserting more fiberfill into the body as you go. Cont from (f) to (g) as foll: *Ch 5, sc in next 2 sts; rep from *. After last 2 sc, end the tail with ch 7, for a final longer point, and anchor work with sc in next st. Weave in loose ends. Working on the very edge of an ironing board, steam-press dragon points, but do not press the stuffed body. Use your fingers to pinch the points into sharp tips. Let dry.

ASSEMBLY

Brim: Fold crown in half and mark center front and center back. Place center of brim onto center front crown, ½" (1.3 cm) up from lower edge of crown. With double strand of mahogany and using a whipstitch, sew brim in place. With single strand of mustard, work a decorative line of crochet chain st embroidery (see page 127) through both brim and crown layers, working about ¼" (6 mm) from top edge of brim.

Neck protector and wings: Mark neck protector piece center back and again at 6" (15 cm) from each front edge along inner curve. Match center back and pin 6" (15-cm) marks just barely overlapping brim. Ease neckpiece inner curve onto crown and pin in place. With single strand of yarn to match neckpiece and using a whipstitch, sew neckpiece to crown. Mark halfway between center front and center back on each side, about 3½" (9 cm) to 4" (10 cm) up from neckpiece sewn edge. Fold side wings back to marked points and secure in place by sewing shank buttons through both layers.

Tassel: Mark center back of crown 2" (5 cm) down from mustard purl ridge at top. Fold tassel cord in half. Make a loop at fold, and with one strand of mustard threaded on a tapestry needle, work whipstitches very close together to sew in place about 1" (2.5 cm) down from fold. Fold both ends through loop (Figure 1) and gently pull ends down (Figure 2) toward the neckpiece.

Dragon: Thread tapestry needle with single strand of mustard and whipstitch dragon at nose, belly, and tail to front of crown.

CROCHET CHAIN STITCH EMBROIDERY

DRAGON

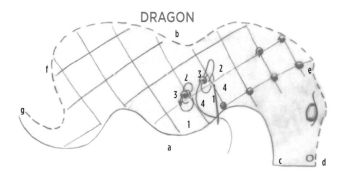

Figure 1

Nose

Tail

Figure 2

TASSEL

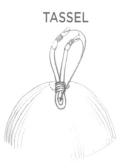

Figure 1

Figure 2

Abbreviations

beg	beginning; begin; begins
bet	between
BO	bind off
CC	contrast color
cm	centimeter(s)
cn	cable needle
CO	cast on
dec(s)	decrease(s); decreasing
dpn	double-pointed needles
g	gram(s)
inc	increase(s); increasing
k	knit
k1f&b	knit into the front and back of same st
k2tog	knit 2 sts together
k3tog	knit 3 sts together
kwise	knitwise, as if to knit
LC	left cross
m	marker(s)
MC	main color
mm	millimeter(s)
M1	make one increase
p	purl
p1f&b	purl into front and back of same st
p2tog	purl 2 sts together
p3tog	purl 3 sts together
patt(s)	pattern(s)
psso	pass slipped st over
p2sso	pass 2 slipped sts over
pwise	purlwise, as if to purl
RC	right cross

rem	remain(s); remaining
rep	repeat(s); repeating
rev St st	reverse St st
rnd(s)	round(s)
RS	right side
sl	slip
sl st	slip st (slip 1 st pwise unless otherwise indicated)
ssk	slip 2 sts kwise, one at a time, from the left needle to right needle, insert left needle tip through both front loops and knit together from this position (1 st decrease)
sssk	slip 3 sts kwise, one at a time, work as above through 3 sts instead of 2 (2 st decrease)
ssp	slip 2 sts kwise, one at a time, from left needle to right needle, insert left needle tip through both front loops and transfer both back to left needle in turned position. Working through back loops of both sts, insert right needle from left to right and purl both together.
sssp	slip 3 sts kwise, work as above through 3 sts instead of 2 (2 st decrease)
st(s)	stitch(es)
tbl	through back loop
tog	together
WS	wrong side
wyb	with yarn in back
wyf	with yarn in front
yo	yarn over
*	repeat starting point
* *	repeat all instructions between asterisks
( )	alternate measurements and/or instructions
[ ]	instructions are worked as a group a specified number of times.

Glossary and Techniques

BIND-OFFS

BASIC BIND-OFF

Knit two stitches, *insert left needle tip into first stitch on right needle (Figure 1) and lift this stitch up and over the second stitch and off the needle (Figure 2). Repeat from * for the desired number of stitches.

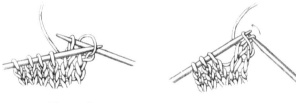

Figure 1   Figure 2

SLOPED BIND-OFF

On the row preceding the bind-off row, do not work the last stitch. Turn work—there will be one stitch on the right needle. Place working yarn in back, slip the first stitch on left needle purlwise (Figure 1), use left needle tip to lift the unworked stitch over the slipped stitch and off the needle (Figure 2) to bind off one stitch. Knit the next stitch and continue binding off as for the basic bind-off method.

Figure 1   Figure 2

THREE-NEEDLE BIND-OFF

Place the stitches to be joined onto two separate needles and hold the needles parallel so that the right sides of knitting face together. *Insert a third needle into the first stitch on each of two needles (Figure 1) and knit them together as one stitch (Figure 2), knit the next stitch on each needle the same way, then use the left needle tip to lift the first stitch over the second and off the needle (Figure 3). Repeat from * until one stitch remains on third needle. Cut yarn and pull tail through last stitch to secure.

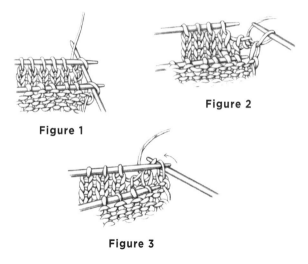

Figure 1   Figure 2

Figure 3

BLOCKING

Blocking is the process of wetting or steaming knitted pieces to even out the lines of stitches and the yarn fibers. There are a number of ways to do this.

STEAM-BLOCKING

Hold an iron set on the steam setting ½" (1.3 cm) above the hat and direct the steam over the entire surface, *except* the ribbing (if there is any). You can get similar results by placing wet cheesecloth on top of the hat and repeatedly touching a dry iron lightly to the wet cheesecloth—do not move the iron across the cheesecloth. Let the hat dry completely before moving it.

WET-BLOCKING

Spray hat with water, pat it into shape, and let it dry.

WET-TOWEL BLOCKING

Run a large bath or beach towel through the rinse/spin cycle of a washing machine to thoroughly moisten it. Roll the hat in the damp towel, place the roll in a plastic bag, and leave it to set overnight. The hat will be uniformly damp and ready to shape the next morning.

CAST-ONS

BACKWARD LOOP CAST-ON

*Loop working yarn counterclockwise and place this loop on the needle so that it doesn't unwind. Repeat from * for desired number of stitches.

CABLE CAST-ON

*Insert right needle between first two stitches on left needle (Figure 1), wrap yarn around needle as if to knit, draw yarn through (Figure 2) and place new loop on tip of left needle (Figure 3) so that new loop forms first stitch on needle. Repeat from * for desired number of stitches, always working between the first two stitches on the left needle.

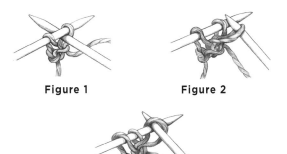

Figure 1   **Figure 2**

Figure 3

CROCHET CHAIN PROVISIONAL CAST-ON

With a crochet hook and waste yarn, make a crochet chain (see page 131) 4 stitches longer than the number of stitches you want to cast on. With knitting needle and working yarn, pick up and knit one stitch through the back loop of each chain stitch (Figure 1) for every stitch to be cast on. When you're ready to work in the opposite direction, pull out the crochet chain and carefully place live stitches on a needle.

Figure 1   **Figure 2**

LONG-TAIL CAST-ON

Leaving a long tail (about ½" to 1" [1.3 to 2.5 cm] for each stitch to be cast on), make a slipknot and place on right needle. Place thumb and index finger of left hand between yarn ends so that working yarn is around your index finger and tail end is around your thumb. Secure ends with your other fingers and hold palm upwards, making a V of yarn (Figure 1). Bring needle up through loop on thumb (Figure 2), grab first strand around index finger with needle, and go back down through loop on thumb (Figure 3). Drop loop off thumb and, placing thumb back in V configuration, tighten resulting stitch on needle (Figure 4).

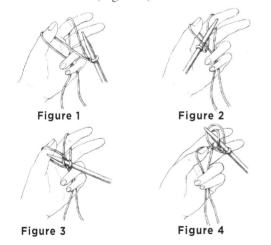

Figure 1   **Figure 2**

Figure 3   **Figure 4**

TWO-COLOR LONG-TAIL CAST-ON

Holding two colors of yarn together (color A and color B), make slipknot and place on right needle as for regular long-tail method (the slipknot will be worked as a single stitch in the next row). Hold the two strands of A as for the regular long-tail method, with the tail over your thumb and the working yarn over your index finger, and cast on 1 stitch. Drop both strands of A so that each strand is on the outside edge of color B. *Pick up

both strands of B through the center (as illustrated) and cast on 1 stitch. Drop both strands of B to the outside, pick up A through the center, and cast on 1 stitch. Repeat from * for one less than the desired number of stitches (the slipknot counts as the final stitch). *Note:* The yarns will twist around each other and you may need to stop periodically and untwist them.

CROCHET

CROCHET CHAIN (CH)

Make a slipknot and place on crochet hook. *Yarn over hook and draw the loop through the slipknot. Repeat from * for desired number of stitches. To fasten off, cut yarn and draw end through last loop formed.

SINGLE CROCHET (SC)

*Insert crochet hook into an edge stitch, yarn over hook and draw a loop through the stitch, yarn over hook (Figure 1), and draw loop through both loops on hook (Figure 2). Repeat from * for desired number of stitches.

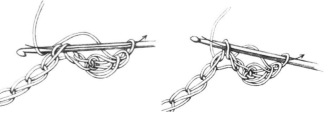

Figure 1   **Figure 2**

SLIP-STITCH CROCHET (SL ST)

Insert hook into stitch, yarn over hook, and draw loop through stitch and loop on needle (Figure 1).

Figure 1

DOUBLE CROCHET (DC)

Yarn over hook, insert hook into a stitch, yarn over hook and draw a loop through (three loops on hook), yarn over hook (Figure 1) and draw it through two loops, yarn over hook and draw it through the remaining two loops (Figure 2).

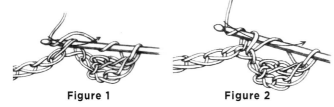

Figure 1   **Figure 2**

TRIPLE CROCHET (TC)

Wrap yarn around hook two times, insert hook into a stitch, yarn over hook and draw a loop through (four loops on hook; Figure 1), yarn over hook and draw it through two loops (Figure 2), yarn over hook and draw it through the next two loops, yarn over hook and draw it through the remaining two loops (Figure 3).

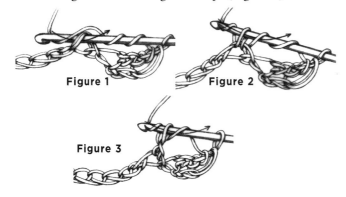

Figure 1   **Figure 2**

Figure 3

DECREASES

SLIP 1, KNIT 1, PASS SLIPPED STITCH OVER (SKP OR SL 1, K1, PSSO)

Slip one stitch knitwise, knit the next stitch, then use the left needle tip to lift the slipped stitch (Figure 1) over the knitted stitch and off the needle (Figure 2).

Figure 1   **Figure 2**

SLIP 1, KNIT 2 TOGETHER, PASS SLIPPED STITCH OVER (SK2P OR SL 1, K2TOG, PSSO)

Slip one stitch knitwise, knit the next two stitches together, then use the left needle tip to lift the slipped stitch over the stitch formed after knitting two stitches together (see above).

SLIP, SLIP, KNIT (SSK)

Slip two stitches individually knitwise (Figure 1), then insert left needle tip into front of these two slipped stitches, and use the right needle to knit them together through their back loops (Figure 2).

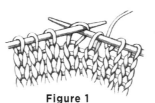

Figure 1   **Figure 2**

SLIP, SLIP, PURL (SSP)

Holding yarn in front, slip two stitches individually knitwise (Figure 1), then slip these two stitches back onto left needle purlwise (they will appear twisted), and purl them together through their back loops (Figure 2).

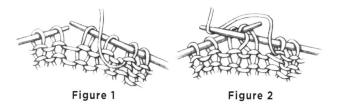

Figure 1 **Figure 2**

VERTICAL DOUBLE DECREASE
(ALSO CALLED CENTERED DOUBLE DECREASE)

Slip two stitches together knitwise to right needle (Figure 1), knit the next stitch (Figure 2), then use the left needle tip to lift the two slipped stitches over the knitted stitch and off the needle. The decreases will form a raised line of stitches (Figure 3).

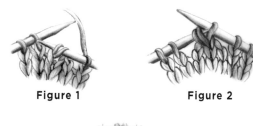

Figure 1 **Figure 2**

Figure 3

EMBROIDERY/EMBELLISHMENTS
COUCHING EMBROIDERY

With yarn threaded on a tapestry needle, make a series of long straight stitches parallel to each other and about ½" (1.3 cm) apart. Work another series of straight stitches on top of and at right angles to the previous ones. Use small stitches to couch the intersections of the two lines of parallel stitches.

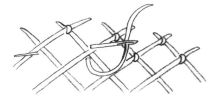

FRENCH KNOT

Bring threaded needle through fabric from back to front, wrap yarn around needle three times, then insert needle back into fabric very close to where it emerged (designated by an x in illustration below), and use your thumb to hold the wraps in place as you pull the needle through to the wrong side of the fabric.

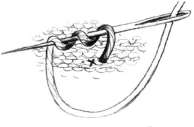

RUNNING STITCH

Bring threaded needle in and out of fabric to form a dashed line of stitches.

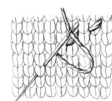

STEM STITCH

(Also called outline stitch) Keeping the working yarn above the needle, bring threaded needle through fabric from back to front, then insert it a short distance to the right, and bring it out again close to the first stitch.

TASSEL WRAP

Cut a strand of yarn about 36" (91.5 cm) long. Lay one cut end of the yarn parallel to the tassel strands. Fold the cut yarn back on itself to create a loop beyond where you want the wrap to end (this will secure the end of the yarn), and beginning at the cut end, wrap the yarn snuggly around the tassel, placing the wraps right next to each other so that none of the tassel shows through (Figure 1). When desired length of wrap is reached, pull the second cut end through the foundation loop until it lies smoothly, finishing the wrap. Pull on first cut end to pull foundation loop to center of wrap (Figure 2). Trim ends of wrapping yarn.

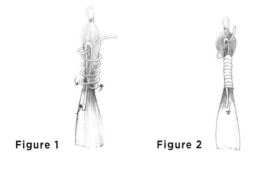

Figure 1   **Figure 2**

FELTING

MACHINE FELTING

Put knitted hat in washing machine with a pair of blue jeans and a tennis shoe or a few tennis balls to increase agitation. Let the washer go through a hot wash/cold rinse cycle. Wash twice for extra body.

HAND FELTING

Fill a basin with very warm but not scalding water. Add soap to the hot water, mix, than add the knitted hat. Scrub, twist, and agitate the hat for several minutes to get the fibers to mat together. Rinse in cold water. Repeat, adding hot water to soapy basin, and rinse in a fresh basin of cold water until hat is desired size. Roll hat in dry bath towel to remove excess water. Shape and let dry according to pattern instructions.

GAUGE

WORKING A GAUGE SWATCH IN THE ROUND

There are several ways you can work a gauge swatch for a project that is worked in the round. The key is that the right side of the work is facing outward in projects worked in the round, so for some stitch patterns—such as stockinette stitch—purl stitches are never worked. Many knitters have different tensions on knit and purl stitches, and this difference can make a difference in the final gauge between a piece worked back and forth in rows and a piece worked in the round. Use the method below that gives you the best approximation of what your knitting looks likes when you work in the round.

Option 1: Using an 11" (28 cm) or 12" (30.5-cm) circular needle, cast on enough stitches to fill the entire needle circumference. For example, if the gauge requires 20 stitches for 4" (10 cm), cast on three times that amount (60 stitches) to accommodate the 12" (30.5-cm) needle, adding stitches if necessary to accommodate full repeats of the stitch pattern you're working. Join, and work in the round, just as you will for the project, until the piece measures at least 4" (10 cm) long. This method produces a large swatch that you may want to keep for future reference.

Option 2: Using a set of 4 or 5 double-pointed needles, cast on the number of stitches required for 4" (10 cm), adding stitches if necessary to accommodate full repeats of the stitch pattern you're working. Join, and work in the round until the piece measures at least 4" (10 cm) long.

Option 3: Using circular needle, cast on 10 more stitches than required for 4" (10 cm), adding stitches if necessary to accommodate full repeats of the stitch pattern you're working. Do not join for working in the round. Beginning with Row 1, work in pattern across all of the stitches on the needle. Without turning the work, slide all of the stitches to the opposite end of the needle and loosely loop the yarn across the back of the work. Work across all of the stitches on the needle again, this time following Row 2 of the pattern. Continue in this manner, always working with the right-side of the work facing you, always slipping the stitches to the opposite needle tip at the end of the row, and always looping the working yarn across the back of the work. The edge stitches will loosen due to the stranded yarn across the back of the work, so be sure to measure gauge in the middle of the work. This gauge swatch is usually raveled and the yarn is reused.

INCREASES

BAR INCREASE KNITWISE (K1F&B)

Knit a stitch but leave it on the left needle (Figure 1), then knit through the back loop of the same stitch (Figure 2) to make two stitches from one (Figure 3).

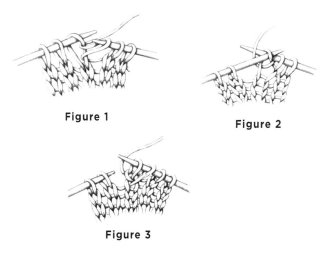

Figure 1

Figure 2

Figure 3

BAR INCREASE PURLWISE (P1F&B)

Purl a stitch but leave it on the left needle (Figure 1), then purl through the back loop of the same stitch (Figure 2) to make two stitches from one. *Note:* You may find it easier to work through the back loop first, then work through the front loop.

Figure 1

Figure 2

LIFTED INCREASE

Left-Slant Knitwise:

Knit into the back (the "purl bump") of the stitch directly below the stitch on the needle (Figure 1), then knit into the stitch on the needle (Figure 2), and slip both stitches off the needle.

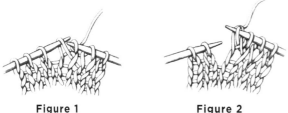

Figure 1   Figure 2

Left-Slant Purlwise:

Insert right needle from top into the purl bump of the stitch below the stitch on the needle (Figure 1), purl this stitch, then purl the stitch on the needle (Figure 2).

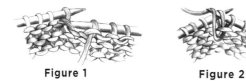

Figure 1   Figure 2

Right-Slant:

Insert left needle tip into back (the "purl bump") of the stitch directly below the stitch just knitted (Figure 1), and knit this stitch (Figure 2).

Note: When working lifted increases with bulky yarn, it helps to create a neater increase if the left needle is inserted into the stitch below from the back, then knitting this lifted stitch through the back loop.

Figure 1   Figure 2

RAISED INCREASE (M1)

If no direction is specified, work the left-slant increase.

Left-Slant (M1L): With left needle tip, lift the strand between last knitted stitch and first stitch on left needle, from front to back (Figure 1), then knit the lifted loop through the back (Figure 2).

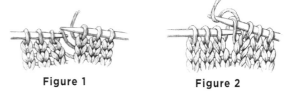

Figure 1   Figure 2

Right-Slant (M1R): With left needle tip, lift the strand between last knitted stitch and first stitch on left needle, from back to front (Figure 1), then knit the lifted loop through the front (Figure 2).

Figure 1   Figure 2

KNITTING METHODS

SHORT ROWS

Work to turn point, slip next stitch purlwise to right needle. Bring yarn to front (Figure 1). Slip same stitch back to left needle (Figure 2). Turn work and bring yarn in position for next stitch, wrapping the stitch with the working yarn as you do so. When you come to wrapped stitch on a subsequent row, hide the wrap by

Figure 1   Figure 2

working it together with the wrapped stitch as follows: Insert right needle tip under the wrap (from the front if wrapped stitch is a knit stitch; from the back if wrapped stitch is a purl stitch), then into the stitch, and work the two together.

FAIR ISLE KNITTING

Fair Isle, or color stranding, is a technique of multi-colored knitting in which yarns that are not in use are carried across the back of the work. In traditional Fair Isle, just two colors are used in a row, the colors are changed frequently, and diagonal pattern lines domi-nate over vertical lines to evenly distribute the tension over the knitted fabric. To work Fair Isle patterns, simply work the designated number of stitches with one color, drop that color, pick up the next color and work the designated number of stitches with that color, drop that color, and so on. This type of knitting is most efficient if the two yarns are held simultane-ously; one in the left hand and worked in the Continental method, the other in the right hand and worked in the English method.

The key to Fair Isle knitting is stranding the unused yarn loosely across the back of the work—the stitches will pucker if the strands are pulled too tightly across the back, ruining the appearance. To prevent this, spread the stitches on the right-hand needle to their approximate gauge each time you change colors rather than allowing them to scrunch up near the tip of the needle.

INTARSIA KNITTING

Intarsia, or jacquard, is a method of knitting that uses isolated blocks of color. These blocks may have vertical, horizontal, diagonal, or curved boundaries. Because the colors are used in limited areas, this type of knitting is most commonly worked back and forth in rows (knit one row, purl one row), not circularly. A separate ball or butterfly of yarn is used for each color block. Tangles are inevitable and you'll need to stop periodically to separate the individual balls or butterflies.

At each color change, twist the yarns around each other to prevent holes in the knitting. Always pick up the new color from beneath the one you've just finished. To change colors along a vertical line, twist the yarns around one another on every row. To change colors along a diagonal line, twist the yarns around one another on every other row.

KNITTED CORD (I-CORD)

With double-pointed needle, cast on the desired num-ber of stitches (usually 3 or 4). *Without turning the needle, slide the stitches to the other needle point, pull the yarn around the back of the work, and knit the stitches as usual. Repeat from * until cord measures desired length.

Tip: To prevent the first stitch of each row from being too loose, knit the first stitch, place your right index finger on this stitch to stabilize it, then insert the needle into its largest diameter into the second stitch before knitting it.

SEAMS

BACKSTITCH SEAM

With right sides facing together, pin knitted fabric together with edges even. Thread yarn on a tapestry needle and whipstitch edge stitch to secure. *Insert threaded needle through both layers two stitches to the left, then one stitch back. Repeat from *, working right to left in a circular motion.

INVISIBLE WEAVING FOR GARTER STITCH

Place pieces to be seamed side by side, with the right sides facing upward. *Use a threaded tapestry needle to catch the bottom loop of the edge stitch of a knit ridge on one piece, then the top loop of the corresponding knit ridge on the other piece. Repeat from *, alternating from one piece to the other.

INVISIBLE WEAVING
FOR STOCKINETTE STITCH

Place pieces to be seamed side by side, with right sides facing upward. Note that along the selvedge edges a loose stitch alternates every other row with a tight stitch, and that there is a horizontal bar at the base of the V of the small, tight stitch. *Insert a threaded tapestry needle under this bar on one piece, then under the corresponding bar on the other piece, and pull the seaming yarn snuggly to bring the two pieces together. Repeat from *, alternating from one piece to the other.

INVISIBLE WEAVING FOR
REVERSE STOCKINETTE STITCH

Place pieces to be seamed side by side, with right sides facing upward. Begin at lower edge and work upward, row by row as follows: Insert a threaded tapestry needle under the bottom loop of a purl stitch on one side of the seam, then under the top loop of the corresponding purl stitch on the other side of the seam, and pull the seaming yarn snuggly to bring the two pieces together. Repeat from *, alternating from one side to the other. When the seam in completed, turn the work over and whipstitch once over the seam allowance to secure the seam.

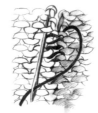

KITCHENER STITCH (GRAFTING)

Place stitches to be joined onto two separate needles. Hold the needles parallel to each other, with the points facing to the right and so that wrong sides of the knitting face each other. With a threaded tapestry needle, work back and forth between the stitches on the two needles as follows:

Step 1: Bring threaded needle through front stitch as if to purl and leave stitch on needle.

Step 2: Bring threaded needle through back stitch as if to knit and leave stitch on needle.

Step 3: Bring threaded needle through the same front stitch as if to knit and slip this stitch off needle. Bring threaded needle through next front stitch as if to purl and leave stitch on needle.

Step 4: Bring threaded needle through first back stitch as if to purl (as illustrated), slip that stitch off, bring needle through next back stitch as if to knit, leave this stitch on needle.

Repeat Steps 3 and 4 until all stitches have been worked.

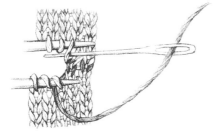

SLIP-STITCH CROCHET SEAM

Make a slipknot and place it on a crochet hook. *Insert hook through both pieces of knitted fabric one stitch in from edge, yarn over hook, and draw loop through fabric and through loop already on hook. Repeat from * for the length of the seam.

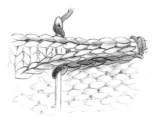

WHIPSTITCH SEAM

Insert threaded tapestry needle at right angle through a stitch on one piece of the work, then through a corresponding stitch on the piece to be attached. Pull stitches together, closing both pieces firmly, but not too tightly.

Sources for Yarns

The following companies supplied the yarns used in this book.

Baabajoes Wool
PO Box 260604
Lakewood, CO 80226
www.baabajoeswool.com
Wool Pak 14-Ply

Brown Sheep Company
100662 Cty. Rd. 16
Mitchell, NE 69357
www.brownsheep.com
Burly Spun
Lamb's Pride Bulky

Cascade Yarns
1224 Andover Park East
Tukwila, WA 98138
www.cascadeyarns.com
Cascade 128 Tweed
Cascade 220
Cascade 220 Tweed
Magnum
Pastaza
Pima Silk
Pima Tencel
Sierra

Classic Elite Yarns
300 Jackson St.
Lowell, MA 01852
www.classiceliteyarns.com
Lush
Montera

Crystal Palace
160 23rd St.
Richmond, CA 94804
www.straw.com/cpy
Cotton Chenille
Deco-Ribbon
Splash

Dale of Norway
N16 W23390 Stone
Ridge Dr., Ste. A
Waukesha, WI 53188
www.dale.no
Free Style
Svale
Tiur
Ull

Habu Textiles
135 West 29th St., Ste. 804
New York, NY 10001
www.habu.com
Shoshoni Paper

Harrisville Designs
Center Village, Box 806
Harrisville, NH 03450
www.harrisville.com
Jasmine
Flax & Wool

JCA Inc.
35 Scales Ln.
Townsend, MA 01469
(978) 597-8794
www.jcacrafts.com
Reynolds Saucy

Louet Sales
808 Commerce Park Dr.
Ogdensburg, NY 13669
www.louet.com
Euroflax Heathers
Chunky
Euroflax Originals

Mountain Colors
PO Box 156
Corvallis, MT 59828
www.mountaincolors.com
Moguls

Muench Yarns Inc.
1323 Scott St.
Petaluma, CA 94954
(800) 733-9276
www.muenchyarns.com
Touch Me

S. R. Kertzer
50 Trowers Rd.
Woodbridge, ON
L4L 7K6
Canada
Naturally Merino
et Soie

Simply Shetland
1338 Ross St.
Petaluma, CA 94954
(707) 762-3362
www.unicornbooks.com
Jamieson's Soft Shetland

Bibliography

Albrizio, Ann, and Osnat Lustig. *Classic Millinery Techniques.* Asheville, North Carolina: Lark Books, 1998.

Arnoldi, Mary Jo, and Christine Mullen Kreamer. *Crowning Achievements, African Arts of Dressing the Head.* University of California, Los Angeles: Fowler Museum of Cultural History, 1995.

Ayo, Yvonne. *Eyewitness Books: Africa.* London: DK Children, 2000.

Fagg, William. *Yoruba Beadwork, Art of Nigeria.* New York: The Pace Gallery, 1980.

Fairservis, Jr., Walter A. *Costumes of the East.* Riverside, Connecticut. The Chatham Press Inc., 1971.

Fox, Lilla M. *Folk Costume of Western Europe.* Boston: Plays Inc., 1971.

Kennett, Frances. *Ethnic Dress. London: Mitchell Beazley, 1995.*

Kilgour, Ruth Edwards. *A Pageant of Hats, Ancient and Modern.* New York: Robert M. McBride Co., 1958.

McDowell, Colin. *Hats, Status, Style, and Glamour.* New York: Rizzoli, 1992.

Pang, Guek-Cheng. *Kazakhstan.* New York: Marshall Cavendish, 2001.

Peacock, John. *Costume 1066–1966.* London: Thames and Hudson Ltd., 1986.

Reynolds, William, and Ritch Rand. *The Cowboy Hat Book.* Salt Lake City, Utah: Gibbs Smith, 1995.

Wilcox, R. Turner. *The Dictionary of Costume.* New York: Charles Scribner's Sons, 1969.

Acknowledgments

A beautiful piece of knitted fabric requires that each and every stitch work in concert with the stitches around it to produce a reliable and stable fabric, one with integrity in its purpose. So it is with writing this book. I am just one stitch among the whole, and I have relied on each and every other person involved for their unique and necessary contribution. My thanks are stated briefly, but are heartfelt and without reservation.

I am always grateful to the founder and visionary of Interweave Press, Linda Ligon, for believing in me and giving me opportunity, and to Marilyn Murphy for continuing her legacy. Ann Budd, you are gracious, thorough in your guidance and technical editing, and always encouraging. Linda Stark, marketing maven and an incredible professional, Betsy Armstrong, editorial director, Stephen Beal, copy editor, and Pauline Brown, production coordinator: I thank you, team Interweave, for helping make *Folk Hats* a reality. Jean Lampe, thanks for sharing your technical editing genius with me! Your expertise is second to none.

To all the knitters who helped me work samples of hats, in part or whole: I could not have done it without your willingness and enthusiasm. Thank you, Joan Pickett, my "right-hand knitter" for working closely with me and trying anything I designed, sometimes more than once, and with nary a complaint! Alice Bush, Lois Eynon, Kathy Hartmeister, Trudy Owen, Micky Shafer, Elaine Sipes, and Sally Thieszen: Your knitting and attention to detail are invaluable!

Thank you to all the models, for sharing your beautiful smiles and having fun modeling all my hats, whether silly or serious! Thank you, Ryan Cannon, Evan Gravdahl, Kristen Heckman, Miles Hilbert, Brett Lambert, Evan Skog, Alex and Justine Square, and A. J. Williams. Ann Swanson, I'm grateful for your creative photostyling. And, of course, Joe Coca: Your photography is fabulous.

My appreciation goes to all the yarn companies who graciously and generously provided yarn. It was thrilling to be able to match my vision of a hat with just the right yarn that brought it to life.

Last, but not least, I am grateful to my wonderful family. To Johnny, Justine, and Alex, my husband, daughter, and son: You are always there for me in every way, to love and encourage, to cheer me on, to share the joy. I am blessed indeed.

Index

A

abbreviations 128
Afghanistan 97, 100
anatomy, hat 8

B

Baseball Cap 22–25
Beaded Cloche 97–99
beret 9
bibliography 141
Bolivia 30
Bolivian Derby 30–32
Bowler, William 30
brim 8

C

Cable Braid 74–76
Cameroon 47
Canada 14
China 106, 109
cloche 9
Congo 36
Cordobes 9
Cordobes with Scarf 51–54
Cossack 88–90
Cossack, Big 91–93
Cowboy Hat 9, 19–21
crown 8

D

Dancer's Hat 117–120
Deerstalker Hat 14–18
de Medici, Catherine 58

E

Ecuador 33
England 68

F

fedora 9
Finland 77
Folded Bloom 113–116
Four Winds Hat 82–84
France 58
Frontière 58–61

G

Germany 65
Glengarry 71–73
glossary 129–139
Gondolier's Boater 55–57
Gourd Baby Bonnet 40–4

H

hat forms, making 11
Hunter's Fedora 65–67
Hut Hat 26–29

I

Ireland 74
Italy 55

J

Japan 117, 121

K

Kazakhstan 94
King Edward VI
  Brimmed Beret 68–70
Knot-Topped Calotte 109–112

L

Lapland 82, 85

M

measurements, head 10

N

Netherlands, The 62
Nigeria 40, 43

P

Pakistan 103
Pakul 100–102
Panama Hat 33–35
Peru 26
pillbox 9

R

Raffia Pillbox 36–39
Renaissance Beret 62–64
Ruffled Dignity 47–50
Russia 88

S

samurai 121
Samurai Kabuto 121–127
Sardou, Victorien 65

Scotland 71
sidebands 8
Soft Winter Snowflakes 77–81
sources 140
Spain 51
Stetson, John B. 19
Striped Baby Hat 103–105

T
techniques 129–139
Thailand 113
types, hat 8–9

U
United States 19, 22

V
Velvet Pillbox 94–96

X
Xinjiang Baby Hat 106–108

Y
Yoruba Bird 43–46

Z
Zigs and Zags Stocking Hat 85–87